Available soon:

For more information visit our website
www.oup.com/vsi/

L. Sandy Maisel

AMERICAN POLITICAL PARTIES AND ELECTIONS

A Very Short Introduction

SECOND EDITION

OXFORD
UNIVERSITY PRESS

OXFORD
UNIVERSITY PRESS

Oxford University Press is a department of the University of Oxford.
It furthers the University's objective of excellence in research, scholarship,
and education by publishing worldwide. Oxford is a registered trade mark of
Oxford University Press in the UK and certain other countries.

Published in the United States of America by Oxford University Press
198 Madison Avenue, New York, NY 10016, United States of America.

Library of Congress Cataloging-in-Publication Data
Names: Maisel, Louis Sandy, 1945–
Title: American political parties and elections : a very short introduction /
L. Sandy Maisel.
Description: Second edition. | New York : Oxford University Press, 2016.|
Series: Very short introductions | Includes bibliographical references and index.
Identifiers: LCCN 2016010375 | ISBN 9780190458164 (paperback)
Subjects: LCSH: Political parties–United States. | Elections–United States.
| BISAC: POLITICAL SCIENCE / Political Process / Elections.
Classification: LCC JK1965 .M34 2016 | DDC 324.973–dc23 LC record
available at https://lccn.loc.gov/2016010375

3 5 7 9 8 6 4 2

Printed in Great Britain
by Ashford Colour Press Ltd., Gosport, Hants.
on acid-free paper

This book is dedicated to our grandsons, Conrad, Gus, and Leo Anderson and Weber and Tyler Maisel, with the hope that I can transmit to them the lessons of American parties and elections—for each generation must again commit to upholding the key principles of democracy on which this nation's greatness depends.

Contents

List of illustrations

Preface

The concept of the Very Short Introduction series has intrigued me for some time. You can go to your local bookstore, pick up a volume, and quickly relearn what you once knew but had forgotten about important subjects. Or you can find a volume on something you should know about but never found time to study. I must admit that I have long thought of these books as sophisticated crib notes, written by scholars who understand what is important about a subject and can distill complex information in an accessible format.

Then I was approached to write this book. My admiration for those who have written VSIs on Democracy or Fascism, on Islam or Judaism, on Kant or Socrates, on Choice Theory or Literary Theory has increased immensely. Like John Pinder, one of the authors in this series, I have thought often of the claim—attributed at various times to Dr. Johnson, Twain, Shaw and various other sages—that they wrote a long letter because they did not have time to write a short one.

The difficulty in writing a short work about a subject on which one has written at length is to decide what is essential and what merely interesting, to determine which familiar but complex concepts are intuitively known accurately by your audience and which are often misunderstood, to choose when familiar examples are needed to illustrate a process and when a generalized description will suffice; in this revision, I have attempted to give contemporaneous examples while still concentrating on themes that the reader can

apply not only in the immediate context but also into the future. In my case, the difficulty was exacerbated because American political parties and elections are of interest to an American audience familiar in a general way with much of the process, and to a non-American audience to whom the electoral process in the United States is not only unfamiliar but also significantly different from their own.

The importance of understanding how elections work

In my view, the subject matter of this book merits the attention needed to approach these tasks carefully. The electoral process serves as the link between the people and their government. When a government is as powerful as that of the United States, the consequences for all citizens of the world are so high that at least a basic understanding of how those who govern are chosen is essential. Do the decisions of the government in fact represent the will of the people? Do the opinions expressed by elected leaders reflect the views of Americans more generally? If not, why does the system not link the representatives and the represented more closely?

The reader will judge how well I have distilled the complex American electoral process to its core elements and have discussed the implications of these elements for governing. My goal was to accomplish these tasks so that the reader can follow an election and critique the system knowledgeably. More than that, I sought to evaluate the process against rigorous democratic criteria, the principles to which Americans hold dear. I am a passionate believer in American democracy, but I am also an ardent critic. And I do not believe that those two positions are inconsistent. The American electoral process works very well for the United States—but not perfectly. As a nation based on an ideal democratic creed, as eloquently laid out in the Declaration of Independence, the

United States should have a constant goal of improving the ways in which citizens express their consent to those who govern them.

In the pages that follow, I hope to inform the reader about the American system and to stimulate thought and discussion about ways to improve it. Reform is not easy; were it easy to right the problems with the American system, someone would have done so long ago. Consequences of reform efforts are notoriously difficult to predict; passage of reform proposals are always difficult because of those with vested interests in the status quo. But anticipated difficulty does not mean that effort is not worthwhile; that is what striving for an ideal is all about. As Woodrow Wilson, a noted reformer himself, said, "Some people call me an idealist. Well, that is the only way I know to be an American. America is the only idealistic nation in the world."

Acknowledgments

In working on the revision of this book, I have accumulated many debts. I want to thank Tim Bartlett and Kate Hamill, the editors at Oxford who brought this idea to me, and especially Dedi Felman and her assistant, Michele Bove, who have seen it through to completion. My thanks go to Helen Mules, Mary Sutherland, and Jane Slusser for their fine editorial work. I have always considered myself extremely lucky to work at Colby College, an institution that values the two aspects of my professional work from which I derive most enjoyment—undergraduate teaching and productive scholarship.

Many people helped on this first edition of this book, and my debt to Andrea Berchowitz, my research assistant at the time, and to Rhodes Cook, Brooke McNally, Pippa Norris, Dan Shea, Harold Stanley, and Amy Walter remains important to any success this book has had. Bob Atkins, Lynn Bindeman, and especially Helen Irving commented on the manuscript from the perspective of informed non-American readers. Meredith Keenan looked over much of this book and made helpful suggestions for updating changes. Most significantly, Jane Wiesenberg did an amazing job in helping me to revise chapters 5 and 6, incorporating results from and lessons from the three most recent American elections. Of course, all faults that remain are mine alone.

As has been true for more than twenty years, my most significant debt is to my wife, Patrice Franko. When I wrote the first edition of this book, we were both on sabbatical leave. We worked on separate projects during that leave—and on one joint project—without the conflicts some might predict. As I have worked on this revision, she and I have continued to share a wonderful professional and well as personal partnership. My hope is that Patrice feels that my support for her has been as helpful as I know hers has been for me.

The first edition of this book was dedicated to five wonderful friends, Joe Boulos, Bob Diamond, Bob Gelbard, Bill Goldfarb, and Larry Pugh, not only because their loyalty and generosity to Colby College has made my professional home for four decades a better place, but also because they are role models who combine commitment, excellence, and success in their professional lives with devotion to and love of family, enjoyment of leisure time spent with good friends, and commitment to community.

This edition is dedicated to Patrice's and my five grandsons, in hopes that they learn life lessons from role models like those five friends and that they learn to participate in and contribute to American democracy, the great gift to this nation's people from our founders, which requires constant vigilance and re-examination if it is to continue to thrive.

Sandy Maisel
Rome, Maine
July 2015

Chapter 1
The context of American elections and political parties

Americans are proud—justifiably proud, given its longevity—of their democratic electoral system. Yet, truth be told, few Americans and even fewer observers from other nations understand the American electoral process. Most citizens of democratic regimes evaluate other democracies according to the standard set by their own. But representative democracies come in many varieties. What is common across democratic systems is that citizens vote to choose those who are to govern them. In some cases they choose executives, legislators, and judges; in others, only some of these. In some nations, voters choose national, regional, and local officeholders; in others, only some of those. What is critical is that citizens can evaluate the performance of those who make decisions that most directly affect their lives.

The world's democracies are judged to be more or less effective based on a number of factors. Is the process open? Do those out of power have a chance to contest for office successfully? In Canada, party control of government has switched with some frequency. In the old Soviet Union, such power-shifting was unimaginable.

Do citizens participate easily and freely in the political process? In Denmark and Germany, turnout in typical elections for the legislature averages between 70 and 90 percent; in Poland and

Switzerland, about 50 percent; and in recent U.S. elections, around 36 percent have voted in midterm elections and about 50 percent in presidential.

To how much information do citizens have access before they reach their decisions of voting? How free are candidates and parties to express their views on the issues of the day? Democratic regimes span a wide spectrum in terms of how freely those in power can be criticized, by the press or by the opposition, on such issues as the openness of the process, the ability of those out of power to contest for office successfully, the level of participation among the citizenry, the amount of information to which citizens have access in reaching their judgments, and the freedom that candidates have to express their views and that citizens have to vote.

By all of those standards, the democracy in the United States scores quite high. In terms of citizen rights and procedures American democracy is exemplary, but a higher standard is needed. Voters and candidates must be able to take advantage of these procedures and thus exercise their rights in a way that impacts governmental policy to conform with citizens' expressed preferences.

In this book we examine the ways in which the electoral institutions in the United States facilitate, often through voting, the granting of the consent of the governed to those who govern. We also look at *when* this process of generating citizens' support (and thus that consent) for government policy breaks down. Many citizens who care passionately about policy—about the issues of war and peace; economic prosperity; care for the poor, the ill, and the elderly; equal treatment without regard to religion, race, gender, sexual orientation, physical handicap; protection of the environment; and so many others—are bored by the mechanics of the electoral process. But those are the questions that enthrall me. The rules by which elections are run often determine who will win and, therefore, whose policy preferences will be heard. Thus,

understanding what may seem like procedural nuances is necessary to understanding both electoral and policy outcomes.

As a starting point in our examination of American democracy, we begin by discussing the aspects of the constitutional framework in the United States that have relevance not only to the electoral process but also key aspects of the electoral process itself. We will look at how each of these basic aspects of American governing contributes to or detracts from the ability of citizens to give consent to the policies imposed by their government. Familiar concepts such as separation of powers and a federal system help explain how America uniquely solves the problem of democratic consent and thus have important consequences that bear a revisiting.

A federal republic with separation of powers

The two defining characteristics of American democracy are the separation of powers (with constitutionally guaranteed checks and balances) and federalism. While other nations share one or both of these traits, the ways in which they function under the U.S. Constitution are unique. One cannot understand the American system without exploring their significance for politics and governance.

Separation of powers means that the executive, legislative, and judicial powers are housed in separate institutions. If an individual serves in the executive branch, he or she cannot serve in the legislature or on a court. At the level of the national government, two minor exceptions exist. The vice president of the United States (an executive branch elected official) serves as president of the U.S. Senate. His only functions are to preside over the Senate and to cast votes in case of a tie. The chief justice of the United States presides over the Senate in the rare circumstance when the Senate is sitting as a court of impeachment for the president; this has happened only twice in the nation's history.

In governments characterized by separation of powers, the chief executive is elected separately from legislators. In the United States, not only are these officials chosen in separate elections but also their terms of office, as specified in the Constitution—a four-year term for the president, two-year terms for members of the House of Representatives, six-year terms of U.S. senators—also guarantee that they are elected by different electorates. A system with separation of powers is distinguished from a parliamentary system, such as that of Great Britain, in which the prime minister is an elected member of Parliament chosen as leader by his fellow legislators.

The United States is a federal republic in that the nation is made up of distinct geographic subunits that have residual powers. The powers of the government of the United States are specified and limited in the Constitution; the Tenth Amendment to the Constitution specifies that "the powers not delegated to the United States by the Constitution, nor prohibited by it to the states, are reserved to the states respectively, or to the people." These states have their own elected governments, also characterized by separation of powers. They differ from each other in ways that are specified in their own state constitutions.

A federated system with separated governing powers means that the ability of citizens to express their views through elections and the interpretation of elections are both difficult. Should citizens vote to reelect a representative in Congress, of whose job they approve, if they feel that the entire Congress is not performing adequately? If a citizen feels that governmental policies are leading the country in a wrong direction, but the president and the Congress have been at loggerheads over policy direction, how can citizens vote effectively to withhold their consent from future policies? Against whom are they dissenting? The president? The Congress? Or the failure of the two to agree?

In most elections in the American federal system, citizens vote for state officials and federal officials at the same time. If citizens feel

that state government is not meeting their expectations because of actions at the federal level, how do they express those views? Because power is shared between the federal and the state governments, and because no one branch of either government can impose its will on the others, it is difficult to translate even clearly understood citizen preferences into subsequent policy. It is also difficult for citizens to cast blame when no one set of officials is fully responsible for policy outcomes.

The long ballot

First, Americans elect more than 500,000 public officials, more than is the case in any other democracy. We separately elect executives, legislators, and in some cases judges (that varies from state to state), at the federal, state, and local levels. We elect many of them at the same time. For instance, on November 6, 2012, citizens of Rocky Mount, North Carolina, cast their votes for president and vice president, for representative in the U.S. House of Representatives, for governor and lieutenant governor and seven other statewide executive branch officials, five state judges and a number of local judges, for state senator, for state representative, and for candidates for a variety of county or local offices. The so-called long ballot evolved in the nineteenth century as a way to extend democracy, but some claim that our system might have produced too much of a good thing.

Because the presidency is the largest prize in the system, the quadrennial election of the president of the United States dominates all other elections. As a result, citizens concentrate on the presidential election and pay less attention to other elections "down the ballot." Some citizens vote only for those elections at the top and leave other choices blank. This phenomenon is called *falloff* and can amount to more than 25 percent on extremely long ballots.

Those running for less salient offices struggle to gain attention. One campaign technique is to bask in the glory of those above you on the ballot and hope that you can ride to office on their coattails; in 2012

Democratic candidates who sensed that President Obama was popular among their constituents urged the president to visit their districts so that they could be seen as part of his entourage. As a consequence of the long ballot, it is difficult to forge the connection between votes cast for lower offices and citizens consenting to the governing policies of those officials. Rarely are the outcomes of elections near the bottom of long ballots determined by candidates' views and records; factors that should be less significant according to democratic theory—name recognition, ethnicity, geographic proximity of the candidate's home to the voter's, and perhaps party affiliation—are often critical.

...or not so long

The second consequence of a federal system with separation of powers is that all ballots are not equally long; in fact, some might be quite short. Because federal legislators' terms differ in length from that of the president, some legislators are elected at the same time as the president, others are not. Because the fifty states have different governing structures and set their own rules, some state governors and legislatures are elected at the same time as the president, some are not; some are elected at the same time as the Congress in nonpresidential years, others are elected separately.

Which offices are contested at the same time as other offices has important consequences. Many states have changed their laws in recent years, so that their statewide offices are not on the ballot in presidential election years. One would hope that actions such as those would make it easier for citizens to express their views of the actions of those for whom they are voting. State issues, not national issues, should dominate political discussion. But, except for in the five states that hold elections in odd-numbered years, citizens elect federal legislators in the same election as state officials, even in these elections.

Table 1.1 shows the possible electoral scenarios that might face the electorate, with examples cited for each. Turnout in elections held

Table 1.1 Office contests at the top of the ballot

	2016	2017	2018	2019
President/governor/ senator/representative	8 New Hampshire	x	x	x
President/governor/ representative	3 West Virginia	x	x	x
President/senator/ representative	26 Alabama	x	x	x
President/representative	13 Maine	x	x	x
Governor/senator/ representative	x	x	22 New York	x
Governor/representative	x	x	16 Massachusetts	x
Governor/state offices	x	2 New Jersey	x	3 Kentucky
Senator/representative	x	x	9 Utah	x
Representative	x	x	3 Louisiana	x

* These numbers assume no additional vacancies in the Senate due to death or resignation.

in the off year, that is, the year in which a president is not being chosen, is typically 75 percent of that in presidential election years. Most attention is paid to the gubernatorial race when it is atop the ballot. United States Senate and congressional races get most

attention only when no more visible offices are contested at the same time. All state issues gain primacy when no federal elections appear on the same ballot.

Table 1.1 could have been extended to include elections for local office, which in some communities are held separately from all federal and state elections, so that the electorate pays attention to the local issues. However, in those cases, while citizens face shorter ballots, they are asked to go to the polls much more often, with a consequent drop-off in turnout. Citizens in Baton Rouge, Louisiana, where state elections are held separately from federal elections, and local elections are held separately from state elections, were asked to go to the polls eleven times in the 2015–2016 biennium.

Citizens have the right to express their views, but because they are asked to so often, many choose not to exercise the franchise. Thus, frequent elections do not necessarily translate into citizens expressing their consent effectively.

In addition, calculating politicians think carefully about the implications of what offices are to be contested in a particular election before deciding whether to run. For instance, it is easier to raise money if running for U.S. senator if a gubernatorial election is not held in your state in the same year, because candidates for governor would siphon off some of the money otherwise available. Such decisions have little relationship to effective democracy.

Fixed terms with regular elections

An additional consequence of the constitutional provisions that govern American elections, and which distinguish our system from many others, is that the terms of all offices in the United States are set and fixed. Thus, no American government can fall because of failure to respond to a crisis. The electorate does not have the opportunity to express opinions until the expiration of a set term.

To use federal offices as an example, elections are held the first Tuesday after the first Monday in November in even-numbered years, no matter what else is happening in the world. The term of the president is four years; if a president dies in office (or resigns, as was the case with President Nixon), a successor replaces him for the remainder of his term, but no new election is held until the next regularly scheduled date.

President Franklin D. Roosevelt was reelected in 1944; a campaign was run despite the fact that we were engaged in World War II. When he died in April, 1945, his little-known vice president, Harry S Truman, succeeded him, leading the nation in the war effort and postwar period without facing the electorate until November 1948. Congressmen serve fixed two-year terms and U.S. senators,

1. **Harry S Truman takes the oath of office as president of the United States in the Cabinet Room of the White House, following the death of President Roosevelt in April 1945.**

six-year terms; if they die or resign, a successor fills the remaining part of that term, but the regular cycle continues. American governments cannot fall through votes of no confidence; elections cannot be timed to coincide with public opinion or world events.

The electoral system in the United States has a number of other facets that are taken for granted by American citizens but also have important implications for translating popular will into governmental policy. Among these are electing the president through the Electoral College, choosing representatives in single-member districts that are defined geographically, and declaring those with a plurality of the votes cast as the election winner, rather than requiring the support of a majority. Changing any of these might seem undemocratic to many citizens, but in fact each is but one means to the end of effective representation, each a means with implications for democracy that few consider.

The Electoral College system

Americans—and the world—became acutely aware of the Electoral College system for electing the president and vice president of the United States in November 2000. For months following the voting, in an election that seemingly would not end, courts debated whether George W. Bush or Albert Gore would win Florida's twenty-five electoral votes. Despite the fact that Vice President Gore won more popular votes than had then Governor Bush, neither candidate had won enough electoral votes to garner the needed majority without Florida's twenty-five. The election was not decided until the U.S. Supreme Court ruled that recounts should cease and the Florida votes be awarded to George Bush, thus determining that he would be the forty-third president.

If political observers became aware of the Electoral College, they are certainly less knowledgeable about why it exists, how it works, and most importantly what political implications follow from this system. That is what is really important. Yet American democracy

is often defined by and either defended or criticized for the way in which the president is elected. It is essential to understand the Electoral College in order to evaluate American democracy because that feature of the election context determines how candidates campaign, to which voters they appeal, and ultimately how accurately citizen views are reflected in the result of the election.

Why an Electoral College?

Put simply, the Electoral College was invented by the founders of the nation in order to solve political problems that they faced. Constitution writing is complicated business. The most important compromise in drafting the Constitution of 1787 was the so-called Connecticut Compromise that called for a House of Representatives, apportioned by population, and a Senate, with each state sending two senators. This compromise resolved the conflict between those states with large populations and those with small. Congressional representatives were to be popularly elected; the states were to determine how their senators were chosen with the norm at the time of adoption election by the state legislature.

But how was the president to be chosen? By the states? Not if the views of the states with large populations were to be heard. By popular vote? The "democrats" who wrote the Constitution were not that democratic; few were willing to entrust such an important decision to the masses. And even if one were to do so, what about the slaves? The slaveholding states wanted their slaves to count for population purposes—and the nefarious three-fifths compromise, counting each slave as three-fifths of a person for the purpose of representation—solved that problem. But although the slaves counted to increase the slaveholding states' representation in the House, they were not to be allowed to vote. That was the farthest thing from the minds of the founders from those states.

The Electoral College was the resultant compromise. The system was a filter from pure democracy. Each state was to select a number of electors equal to the number of congressmen plus the number of

11

senators (always two); this formula was a compromise between large and small states. Each state was to determine for itself how those electors were to be chosen, a concession to states' rights and a clear means of avoiding the necessity to answer the question regarding the slaves. No elector could hold any other office of trust within the federal government; thus, worthy men without a conflict of interest would be chosen. Each elector was to cast two votes, one for an individual not from his state, an effort to avoid state parochialism as the assumption was that only favorite sons would receive votes without this provision. A majority would be needed to elect a president, preventing domination by one or two states. If no majority occurred, the House of Representatives would choose from among the top three finishers, but each state would have only one vote in this election, again compromising the interest of small and large states. The runner-up would become vice president, assuring that a respected man would be in line for the presidency should anything happen to the president.

When looked at from the perspective of the founding generation and the political problems they faced, the Electoral College can be seen as an amazingly successful invention, one which guaranteed the election of a respected leader without violating any of the hard-fought compromises battled over as the Constitution was drawn. That everyone involved in the process knew that George Washington would be selected under this procedure—and that was the desired result—clearly contributed to the adoption of the procedure that in large part is still in place today. It is difficult to argue, however, that the Electoral College fostered democracy. It was a compromise crafted by a political elite to guarantee a desired result.

The Electoral College in the contemporary context

I am not aware of anyone who today would argue in favor of the Electoral College as the ideal way to select the president. Arguments are often raised against specific changes—in fact, these arguments have prevailed in all recent attempts to scrap the

system—but no one is heard to proclaim, "Thank goodness the founders gave us the Electoral College. It is the best system we could have!" Merely saying that out loud demonstrates how ludicrous it is.

But also few are aware of how the Electoral College actually works—and therefore, of what changes could be made. The functioning of the Electoral College has evolved since the ratification of the Constitution. The most fundamental change followed the development of political parties as campaign organizations. As a result, the earliest candidates ran as tickets with the understanding that one candidate was the presidential candidate and the other, the vice presidential. However, the Electoral College system did not allow for such pairings and resulted in no candidate receiving a majority in 1800. To rectify this problem, the Twelfth Amendment to the Constitution, ratified in 1804, provided that electors vote separately for president and vice president.

The second major change has been the adoption by states of a winner-take-all method of allocating the electors chosen within that state. The Constitution leaves the method of choosing electors to the states. By 1836, reflecting democratizing reforms, all states held popular elections of electors in statewide, not district, voting. Because of the power of political parties, this system led quite naturally to winner-take-all elections for pragmatic reasons. If a state were assured to be in one party's column, then winner-take-all made sense to the party in power; the candidate that controlled the state would gain more by winning. Once supporters of one party adopted this system in their states, supporters of the other party had to follow suit in the states they controlled or lose votes in the process. State parties ran slates of candidates, with the number of potential electors on a slate equal to the number that the state was allowed; supporters routinely voted for all of the slate, guaranteeing the desired winner-take-all result.

In a parallel manner, state legislators in closely divided states realized that if the size of the prize were enhanced—all of the state's electoral votes as opposed to just the margin between those allotted to the winner and those allotted to the loser under another system—candidates would concentrate more on that state. Again, when one such state went to a winner-take-all system, other states were pressured to do the same.

Today, the winner-take-all aspect of the Electoral College system, the most controversial part of the system, is used in forty-eight of the fifty states and in the District of Columbia. Each still is allotted a number of electors equal to the number of representatives plus senators. The citizens of the District of Columbia were given the right to vote for president by the Twenty-third Amendment to the Constitution, ratified in 1961, with the specification that the District of Columbia shall have the same number of electors as the least populous state i.e., three. This allocation of electors means that citizens in the states with smaller populations are slightly overrepresented, even though the absolute number of electors in these states is low.

In all states except for Maine and Nebraska, the plurality winner of the popular vote among the slates of electors pledged to the various candidates receives all of the electoral votes for that state. In these two states, the plurality winner in each congressional district receives one vote, and the winner for the entire state receives the other two. Since these systems were adopted by these two states' legislatures, the same candidate has always won each district. As a consequence, this variation from the normal voting procedure has had no practical impact.

A majority of the Electoral College vote is needed to elect a president and vice president. If no majority exists, the president is elected by the House of Representatives from among the top three finishers, with each state casting one vote and a majority of the states' votes needed to win. In that circumstance the vice president is elected by the Senate.

The significance of the Electoral College system

That the Electoral College system for choosing the chief executive is unique among democracies does not make it significant. In evaluating American democracy, however, the system by which the president is chosen is noteworthy for a number of reasons.

- Because of the two electoral votes given to each state beyond those reflecting the state's population, each citizen's vote does not count equally in presidential voting.

> Californians in 2012 had one electoral vote for each 255,246 voters; Mainers had one vote for each 178,275 voters. California's total was 55 electoral votes, and Maine's, 4.

- Because of the winner-take-all nature of electoral voting, candidates do not campaign frequently in states in which they are assured either victory or defeat; as a consequence, some states and their citizens see active campaigns for the presidency, while others (including some of the largest) see virtually none.

> In Iowa, in 2012 the Romney campaign advertising ran 50% above the national average on a per capita basis; the Obama campaign, 35%. In Wisconsin the comparable numbers were 39% above average for the Romney campaign, 46% for Obama's. By contrast, advertising in California, Texas, and New York were all well below the national average.

- Because electoral votes are cast on a state-by-state basis and not nationally, two candidates with virtually the same vote total might receive significantly different electoral vote counts; the system benefits candidates who are strong in one state or region and weak nationally as opposed to those whose strength nationally is the same but spread evenly among the states.

In 1948 two minor party candidates, Strom Thurmond of the States Rights Party and Henry Wallace of the Progressive Party, each received approximately 2.4% of the vote. Thurmond received 39 electoral votes because his votes were concentrated in southern states. Wallace, whose votes were spread throughout the nation, received none.

- Because the margin of victory in a state does not alter that state's prize, that is, all of its electoral votes, it is possible that the candidate who receives the most votes for president does not win the election, as was the case with Al Gore in 2000.

In addition to President Bush, Rutherford B. Hayes (1876) and Benjamin Harrison (1888) were elected to the presidency despite receiving fewer votes than their opponents.

The system came under a great deal of criticism in 2000, because of the closeness of the result and the fact that Bush was a minority winner. Despite that criticism, however, momentum was not found for a shift to any other system—the district plan as used in Maine and Nebraska, a system of awarding the electors within a state proportionately to the votes received, or, most radically, direct election of the president. As a result, the Electoral College system continues to have strategic implications for running presidential campaigns. Certainly, if one believes that the person who receives the most votes should win, the implications for democracy are evident.

Single-member, geographically defined districts with plurality-winner elections

When Hillary Rodham Clinton moved to New York to run for the U.S. Senate in 2000, she was accused of being a carpetbagger, a

colorful term from the Reconstruction era, referring to Yankees who moved to the South (rolling their belongings into a carpet) for exploitative reasons, with no intention of staying. If Clinton wanted to serve in the Senate, she had to reside in the state from which she ran.

Representatives and U.S. senators must reside within the state that sends them to the House or the Senate. But that is the only constitutional requirement regarding residency. Nothing requires that legislators live within the districts they represent, that only one representative represent each district, nor that gaining a plurality of the votes, that is, one more than the next highest vote getter, is sufficient for victory. Yet these norms have important consequences for American politics—determining, in essence, who may run for a seat in a legislature and who wins. Without these restrictions, it can be argued, the electoral process could produce more accurate reflections of citizen preferences, at least on a national level.

Single-member, geographically defined districts

Americans assume that they will have "their" representative in the legislature; that is, one member will be elected from their district to represent them. While such a system is mandated by federal law for the House of Representatives, multimember districts exist in some states and in many local communities. Why is one system seen as superior to the other? Does one lead to better representation?

The history of single-member districts in the United States is instructive. Single-member districts were discussed at the 1787 Constitutional Convention. In one of his articles presenting the case for ratification of the new Constitution, published as *Federalist 56*, James Madison argued that single-member districts would "divide the largest state into ten or twelve districts and it will be found that there will be no peculiar interests . . . which will not be within the knowledge of the Representative of the district." Essentially, local representatives would understand and therefore could defend local interests.

By the time the party system came into play, it became apparent that single-member districts would allow for better representation of partisan interests; while one party might dominate a state's politics, the other party might have strength in certain geographic regions. Despite these arguments, six of the twenty-eight states with more than one representative in the House were still using at-large elections when Congress passed the Reapportionment Act of 1842, mandating single-member districts. Four of those states ignored the law, which some felt an unconstitutional infringement on states' rights, in the next election, with total impunity.

The Congress continued to pass reapportionment acts every decade; most included requirements for single-member districts. In 1929 the Congress passed a law that set up permanent means for reapportionment; but three years later the Supreme Court, in *Wood v. Broom*, 287 U.S. 1 (1932), ruled that any reapportionment act could have effect only for the decennial reapportionment for which it was enacted. Most states continued to use single-member districts, but as late as the Kennedy years, more than twenty members of Congress were elected from multimember districts.

In 1967 Congress passed, and President Lyndon Johnson signed, a new law prohibiting states from electing representatives in multimember districts, a practice that was being used only by Hawaii and New Mexico at the time of that legislation.

The impetus for the new law was the passage of the Voting Rights Act of 1965, extending the franchise to more black citizens, particularly in the South, and the fear that southern state legislatures would revert to multimember districts as a means of diluting black voting power. In addition, some members feared that the courts would order at-large elections when state legislatures had difficulty redistricting—and that such elections might jeopardize their seats in Congress. The 1967 law remains in effect today.

2. President Lyndon B. Johnson signs the Voting Rights Act of 1965 into law, banning racial discrimination in voting practices by the federal government as well as by state and local governments.

Redistricting laws were thus implemented as a means to improve representation—to allow for representatives to know their constituents in the early days, to permit party members who were in a minority statewide but dominant in some regions to elect representatives, and to assure the influence of newly enfranchised black voters. Do any of these reasons pertain today?

Twenty-first-century congressional districts average nearly 700,000 residents. Whereas the founders' vision was of homogeneous populations in relatively small districts represented by one of their own who knew their interests, many of today's districts have extremely diverse populations—in racial, ethnic, socioeconomic, and religious terms—with heterogeneous views on the issues of the day. In the early days of the Republic, geographic districts were necessitated by the difficulty of traversing long distances; today with air travel and electronic communication, contact with constituents does not require close physical proximity.

While single-member districts were designed to enhance effective and fair representation of partisan interests, today those who draw district lines often do so with the express purpose of restricting competition and guaranteeing the desired partisan result. Partisan gerrymandering, drawing lines for the express purpose of gaining partisan advantage, has been challenged in lawsuits before the Supreme Court, with petitioners claiming their rights of equal representation have been violated. But the Court has not prohibited such gerrymandering, thought by many to be responsible for the lack of competition in congressional races, at least in some of the more populous states.

The use of single-member districts to increase the influence of black voters, deemed an important goal after the passage of the Voting Rights Act four decades ago, is also called into question today. Increased racial diversity in most districts, and the mobility of our population that makes predicting district demographics problematic, both raise the possibility that the means is no longer an effective route to the end.

Yet the norm continues. Even citizens whose state representatives or city councilors are elected in multimember districts cling to the notion that their U.S. congressman should represent their local geographic unit and protect their interests. Should the concept of single-member, geographically defined districts be reexamined? Claims and evidence that this "pillar" of American democracy might in fact be counterproductive toward achieving fair representation, competitive elections, and ultimately improved democracy, meet stiff resistance from a citizenry that sees this relatively recently mandated provision of election law as somehow fundamental to what American democracy entails.

Plurality election winners

Americans believe in majority rule. Except that for the most part election winners are determined by a plurality of those voting, not a majority. If true majority rule were the norm, the results of many

elections might be changed. It is worth questioning whether a more effective representation would be the result.

We have already noted that George W. Bush was elected with fewer votes than his opponent Al Gore, despite the majority provision of the Electoral College system. Nonmajority winners are common in American elections, though losers among those who have won a plurality and did not face a runoff are more rare. Despite the fact that the American system is dominated by two parties, in every election year a number of winners poll fewer than half of the votes—and minor party or independent candidates receive enough votes to hold the balance of power. This result is particularly true in primary elections, elections held to determine a party's nominees, in which more than two candidates often vie for a party nomination.

> Think about Dino Rossi. As the Republican candidate, he lost the 2004 gubernatorial election in Washington State to Democrat Christine Gregoire by just over 100 votes out of 2.8 million votes cast. Neither candidate had a majority. Libertarian candidate Ruth Bennett, whose supporters might be presumed to have favored Rossi over Gregoire, polled over 63,000 votes, only 2.3% but enough to influence the result. If a majority had been required, a runoff election might well have favored Rossi.

Again, changing from the current system of "first-past-the-post" winners, that is, the person with the most votes (a plurality) wins, whether that is a majority or not, strikes many Americans as strange, despite its obvious undemocratic implications. Two alternative systems (with variations) are often examined as ways to alter the current practice.

In many southern states and in scattered locales throughout the rest of the nation, runoff elections are held if a majority winner does not emerge. (In a few areas of the nation runoffs are called for if a

"super-plurality" is not obtained, e.g., if the winner does not achieve at least 40 percent of the vote in the first election.) This practice is more common for primary elections than for general elections; it was put in place in part because the primary was the functional equivalent of the general election in the South for many years when the Democrats dominated southern politics. However, runoffs are not without problems. Turnout is normally much lower in runoff elections than in the first-round election; intense ideological groups tend to dominate, because they are better able to mobilize their share of the electorate. Experience has also shown that minorities fare poorly in runoff elections. And, of course, runoffs are expensive for candidates to contest and for jurisdictions to administer.

More recently reformers have pushed for Instant Runoff Voting (IRV). A variety of alternative means have been proposed to implement a system such as this, but the basic concept is that, in races with more than one candidate, citizens cast votes in which they express their preferences for a first choice, a second choice, and so on. After the voting, if no majority is achieved, the candidate with the least support is eliminated, his or her votes are reallocated to the second-choice preference, and totals are recalculated. In multicandidate fields, this procedure is repeated until a majority winner is declared.

IRV has certain obvious democratic advantages. Spoiler candidates no longer impact the result as they do in plurality elections; at the same time, voters can show their preferences for minor party or independent candidates without fear that such votes will aid the candidate they favor least. Candidates do not have to raise vast sums of money in short periods of time to contest runoffs. And most importantly, majority will prevails. But others point to disadvantages, notably that the procedure seems complicated, especially to an electorate that is not terribly well informed as it is.

IRV is used in Ireland and a number of other democracies. IRV is used in the city of San Francisco, with good results. A number of

states have given municipalities the power to implement such a system should they so desire. To the general public, however, IRV still seems strange. It will be a long time before this "fundamental tenet" of American democracy, plurality winners, is replaced with a system that more closely meets the democratic goal of majority rule to which most Americans profess.

The two-party system

After the 2000 elections, some Americans began to question the efficacy of the Electoral College system. Some questioned the choice they were presented in that election. But few questioned the aspects of the electoral process described above, and even fewer called in question the system that has allowed the Democrats and the Republicans to dominate politics for nearly 150 years. Yet the fact that two—and only two—parties can compete effectively for power in the United States has clear implications for the linkage between citizens and their government.

The American electoral system is frequently described as a two-party system. But political parties are not mentioned at all in the Constitution. No laws mandate that elections be contested by the Democrats and the Republicans. Minor party candidates or independent candidates run for many offices in each election cycle; some of them even win, and many more have an impact on the election's outcome. But two parties do dominate American politics. Of the 535 legislators in Congress in 2015, only Senators Bernie Sanders from Vermont and Angus King from Maine were not either a Democrat or a Republican; only one of the fifty state governors have either a "D" or an "R" next to their name; more than 7,350 of the approximately 7,400 state legislators in the forty-nine states that hold partisan elections for that office are either Democrats or Republicans. (Nebraska's legislature is unique in two ways. First, it has only one house, while all of the others have two. Second, state legislators run without partisan affiliation on the ballot. Nonpartisan elections are much more common at the

municipal level, following the old adage that "there is neither a Republican nor a Democratic way to clean the streets.")

The discussion of the electoral context above says a good deal about why a two-party system has evolved in the United States. First, the presidency is the big prize in the United States. It is either won or lost. The winner-take-all nature of voting for the Electoral College exacerbates this effect. A system characterized by separation of powers, in which the chief executive is chosen by a series of plurality-winner elections, does not allow for coalition governments or electoral deal-making; therefore coalitions are formed *before* votes are cast in order to achieve majority status and win the presidency.

Second, single-member districts with plurality winners for legislative seats have much the same effect. Again, only one winner emerges; votes for minor party candidates are viewed as wasted votes or even counterproductive votes, if the least favored candidate wins because of votes cast for someone with no chance of electoral success. A system of multimember districts with proportional representation would encourage additional parties, because they could achieve some level of electoral success and might be able to form coalitions with like-minded parties in the legislature, but such a system has never existed in this country.

The two parties, while in office, have passed additional measures that go far toward ensuring their continued dominance. Most prominent among these is the system of campaign financing that puts minor parties and their candidates at a significant disadvantage. In a similar vein, the debates during recent presidential campaigns have been administered by a *bipartisan*, not a *nonpartisan*, commission. The commission, co-chaired by former heads of the two major parties, has adopted a series of rules regarding participation by minor party candidates that candidates such as Green Party standard-bearer Ralph Nader thought decidedly unfair. The situation has been compared to the proverbial "fox guarding the chicken coop," especially

by those anxious for minor parties to have more of a say in American politics.

That the system favors two parties does not mean that all Americans are satisfied with the result. In a number of recent presidential elections (particularly those of 1992 and 2000) and in some statewide elections (e.g., the Maine gubernatorial election of 1994, in which Independent Angus King actually beat a prominent Democrat and an up-and-coming Republican) many citizens have expressed dissatisfaction with the choices offered by the two major parties. But to say that there is dissatisfaction is not the same as to say that the system is likely to change. Whether one favors a two-party system or a multiparty system, it is difficult to argue against the proposition that the current institutional context leads almost inevitably to dominance by two parties. And that is different from at least discussing the implications of a two-party system for representation.

At the same time, however, the continued existence of a two-party system does not imply that the electoral system—particularly at the state level—remains stagnant. The American party system is a competitive two-party system nationally; that is, the Republicans and the Democrats are the only competing parties that have a chance to win elections, and the outcome of the election between these two parties is in doubt.

But the nature of their competition has changed. For much of the twentieth century, for example, the South was solidly Democratic, a holdover from the Republicans being viewed as the party of Lincoln that promulgated the Civil War and freed the slaves. The Republican Party did not even exist in much of the South until after the elections of 1964. Today, the Republican Party dominates the South; the Democrats find their strengths in urban centers, particularly on the two coasts and in the industrial Midwest.

After the 1960 elections all 22 U.S. senators from the southern states and 99 of the 106 U.S. representatives were Democrats; after 2014, 19 of the 22 senators and 104 of the 143 representatives (the number had increased as a result of population shifting to the region) were Republicans.

While the two major parties contest for offices in all states, tremendous variation exists, both between states and by region within states. Illinois, for example, is competitive statewide, but Chicago is dominated by the Democrats, and downstate by the Republicans. New York is generally quite safe for the Democrats, in normal circumstances, but competitive elections abound in many of the rural areas. And these patterns clearly changed over time and are responsive to the political issues of the day and to the mobility of the population. Nuance is often lost in overgeneralizing about any aspect of American politics.

Summary

Understanding the implications of the framework and rules under which elections are run is critical to appreciating how well the electoral system achieves the ultimate democratic goal—allowing the citizens to express their consent to the officials who govern them and, by implication, to the policies implemented by those officials. The American creed is laid out in the Declaration of Independence, which outlines the basic tenets of democracy, the "self evident truths" upon which democracy in the United States is based and which have been continuously professed since the founding. The most basic truth is that "all men are created equal" and that they are "endowed by their Creator with certain inalienable rights." The purpose of the government is to secure those rights; and the power of the government depends on the consent of the people.

How the people give that consent is determined by the electoral process. And how the electoral process functions, how effectively it

facilitates the people granting their consent to those who govern, is determined by the institutional framework laid out in the Constitution. The most important aspects of that framework are the separation of powers, with a single executive separate from and elected separately from the legislature, and the federal system with residual powers left to the states. The initial means of choosing leaders followed from these elements that were central to the Constitution. The current political system—and the role played by political parties in that system—evolved from those original decisions. To understand the current system and to evaluate American democracy in today's world, it is necessary first to look at that evolution.

Chapter 2
A brief history of American political parties

In *Federalist 10*, written in 1787 to convince the citizens of New York to ratify the new federal Constitution, James Madison, credited most often with proposing the principal outline of the Constitution, warned his readers of the evils of factions, "adverse to the rights of other citizens and to the permanent and aggregate interests of the community." In his Farewell Address to the nation, delivered on leaving the presidency, George Washington warned "in the most solemn manner against the baneful effects of the spirit of party."

Yet it was Madison who urged Thomas Jefferson to join in organizing against the policies of Alexander Hamilton, Washington's secretary of the treasury, the reputed author of the Farewell Address. How ironic that these founders of the nation who feared factions, who argued against political parties, became the leaders of the first parties. The Jeffersonian Democratic-Republicans were really the first modern political party.

The institution that the founders feared had not really been developed at the time of their warnings. But parties—and a two-party system—did develop early in American history and have persisted since. There are historical reasons for the two-party system and for the development of the institution of party.

3. John Adams, Gouverneur Morris, Alexander Hamilton, and Thomas Jefferson, political leaders of the early American republic, were among the founders of the nation's first political parties.

The first American political parties

Madison and Jefferson joined together to organize a political party not because they sought power for themselves but because they believed that Hamilton was leading the country in the wrong direction. Hamilton's economic policies favored the mercantile interests of New England; Madison and Jefferson viewed the nation as rural, exemplified by those on Virginia plantations and the farmers on the western frontier. Each camp felt that it defined the public good.

And therein was the debate. The parties that they formed were the parties of eighteenth-century Anglo-Irish philosopher-politician Edmund Burke ("a body of men united, for promoting by their joint endeavors the national interest"). The founding generation,

as theorists, feared factions and the division in the nation that factions implied. The founding generation, later as those attempting to govern, found that parties were necessary to form the coalitions required to further their views of the common good.

Alexander Hamilton believed that a strong central government was necessary for the new nation to survive, both economically and geopolitically. As treasury secretary in the nation's first years, he had the ear of President Washington, particularly on the critical issues of fully funding the debt incurred during the Revolutionary War and the federal government's assuming the debts that the various states incurred. John Adams, Washington's vice president and eventual successor, agreed with many of Hamilton's views, even though he despised him personally. Thomas Jefferson, Washington's secretary of state, strongly opposed Hamilton's program but remained in the cabinet out of loyalty to Washington. In Congress, however, the division between followers of Hamilton's ideas and those of Jefferson's concept of a more rural, state-centered nation became apparent. The partisan divide grew out of philosophical differences concerning the direction the nation should take.

The dichotomy between the party of Washington, Adams, and Hamilton, known as the Federalists, and the party of Jefferson and Madison, the Democratic-Republicans, became permanent during the debate over adoption of the pro-British Jay Treaty. Jefferson, a Francophile, opposed it. He resigned his cabinet post and returned to Monticello, his Virginia home. But not for long.

Washington announced that he would not seek a third term in 1796. John Adams, as vice president, sought to succeed him, intent on following through with Hamilton's program, without the presence of Hamilton himself. Congressional opponents of Hamilton's views organized a campaign for Jefferson by writing to

their constituents for support. Adams narrowly beat Jefferson in the election, by three electoral votes; Jefferson conceded to Adams and agreed to serve as his vice president, as specified by the electoral process at that point, an important step in nation building as he acknowledged the legitimacy of the electoral system. This party system was policy-centered and formed at the seat of the national government, spreading to the far reaches of the nation.

Adams proved to be an unpopular leader, and Jefferson opposed him again in 1800. The party system was mature enough by that time that all of the electors favoring Jefferson also cast their second vote for his choice of running mate, Aaron Burr—and they tied for the presidency, each polling eight more electoral votes than Adams. Under the constitutional provisions in place then, because no candidate had received a majority of the electoral votes, the election was thrown into the Federalist-controlled House of Representatives to decide among the top three finishers, and the country was in a crisis, rife with rumors of clandestine deals to keep the presidency from Jefferson. Jefferson was eventually elected, after thirty-five inconclusive ballots in the House. Because the winner of the election was not denied his prize, the legitimacy of the electoral process was established.

The contributions of these early years to nation building are truly astounding, and the parties, reviled by the founders before they came to power, played a major role. First, a popular president, who could easily have been reelected as long as he wanted, voluntarily relinquished power in 1796. Then, after the election to succeed him, a candidate who opposed the policies of the president and was narrowly defeated agreed to serve as vice president, because that was the constitutional stipulation in place at the time. Third, a party system formed through which national leaders were able to take their policy differences to the electorate, for the voters to decide. Of course, the electorate was miniscule in those days—and restricted to white males and in many states property owners.

4. The heated political rivalry between Aaron Burr and Alexander Hamilton ended in a duel at Weehawken, New Jersey, on July 11, 1804.

Fourth, in 1800 the incumbent president lost the election and eventually conceded, though it would have been possible for him to stay in power through manipulating the House of Representatives. When Adams voluntarily turned over the power of the presidency to Jefferson, the legitimacy of the new nation's political system was assured; and the role that parties were to play in that system demonstrated a primacy without precedent.

Soon after the election of 1800, the Federalists became little more than a New England sectional party. Their policies were too conservative to appeal to the nation, and their leaders made little effort to compromise in order to gain popularity. Anglophiles to the end, they opposed Congress's declaration of war against Britain

in 1812. By 1820 the Democratic-Republicans were without major challengers.

The first party period in American history ended with the disappearance of the Federalists. Today Americans would be amazed if a major party were to vanish, but remember, these were fragile and immature parties. Citizens had not had time to develop loyalty to a party as an institution—their loyalty was to the leaders. The political elite were not divided on every issue. It was Jefferson, in his first inaugural address, who said, "Every difference of opinion is not a difference of principle. . . . We are all Republicans, we are all Federalists." Legislators' loyalties were more to region than to party. Jefferson as president used to hold carefully orchestrated dinner parties in order to cajole congressmen to support his views. When Federalist leaders failed to respond to popular dissatisfaction with their views, there was no ingrained party organization to uphold the party. The leaders retired back to their homes, and the party disappeared.

The development of modern parties

The development of modern political parties over the last 200 years can be viewed from different analytical frameworks. Each adds to our understanding of the role that party plays in American politics today.

Parties as a reflection of policy divisions among the electorate

The ideological and policy split between the Federalists and the Democratic-Republicans defined partisanship during the early years of the American republic. When the Federalists disappeared as a threat to win a national election, that division also disappeared. During the "era of good feelings" following the demise of the Federalists, electoral competition was found within the Democratic-Republicans.

All four candidates who ran in the election of 1824—John Quincy Adams, Henry Clay, William J. Crawford, and Andrew Jackson— were Democratic-Republicans; the party did not choose one nominee. The story of that election is a fascinating one, too complex to relate here. Suffice it to say that Andrew Jackson won the most popular votes and the most electoral votes in the election, but he did not receive a majority of the electoral votes, so the election was thrown to the House of Representatives. There, Speaker of the House Henry Clay, who had finished fourth in the Electoral College voting and thus had been eliminated, threw his support to John Quincy Adams, who was elected as the sixth president. Adams then named Clay as his secretary of state, raising claims from the Jackson camp of a corrupt bargain.

Party labels and loyalties remained volatile during this period. In 1828, Jackson, running as a Democratic-Republican, challenged President Adams, the candidate of the National Republicans, and easily defeated him. The election was based on personality more than issues. And with victory, the Jackson party, soon to be known simply as the Democrats, garnered the spoils of victory, claiming all government patronage jobs for their own, throwing out supporters of Adams.

However, the burning issue of slavery, as exemplified by the Missouri Compromise, was emerging beneath this politics of personality and patronage. Party politics in this era can be understood by how the political elite responded to the slavery question. The Whig party replaced the National Republicans as the main opposition to the Democrats from 1836 through 1852, but both parties equivocated on the issue of slavery. Third parties, first the Liberty party and then the Free-Soil party, emerged as alternatives to the major parties, facing up to the most important issue of the day. In 1854 the Republican party was formed as a major alternative to the Democrats, confronting them on the issue of slavery. By 1856 the Whigs had all but disappeared, with former president Millard Fillmore receiving only eight electoral votes as

their standard-bearer, losing to Democrat James Buchanan and the first Republican candidate for president, James C. Fremont. In 1860 Abraham Lincoln won the presidency as a Republican, defeating a Democratic party that was split between its northern and southern camps.

The Missouri Compromise

The nation—and thus the Senate—was divided equally between free states and slave states, with the abolition movement starting to gain momentum in the North. When the Missouri Territory applied for statehood, northerners first insisted on a clause barring the importation of slaves to the new state. This clause was rejected in the Senate in a debate that foreshadowed the bitterness that was to characterize the debate on slavery for decades to come. The Missouri Compromise of 1820 ended the nation's first crisis on the slavery issue, admitting Maine as a free state at the same time that Missouri was admitted with slaves, but the issue of slavery dominated politics for the next four decades.

The Democrats and the Republicans have dominated American electoral politics as the two major parties since that time. No other party's candidate has won the presidency; no other party's followers have gained majority status in Congress. But that is not to say that party politics has remained dormant for 150 years. The issues that have divided the parties and the compositions of their electoral coalitions have changed again and again.

For decades after the Civil War, and particularly after the end of Reconstruction in 1876, when the Democrats made serious inroads into the South because of lingering resentment toward the party of Lincoln, national partisan battles were closely fought. In a time of rapid industrialization in the nation, the leaders of industry dominated both parties. They backed candidates, many of them generals from the Civil War, who would support their programs of economic advancement. Immigrants flooded the nation's shores and

supported the party that was in power in the urban centers to which they moved, because that party, tied to the area's industrialists, would guarantee jobs and security. As the nation grew into an industrial power, policy debates took a backseat to power politics.

A series of seemingly unrelated events prevented the Republicans from total domination during this period. First, scandals and an economic depression rocked the administration of Ulysses S. Grant (1869–77), held down Republican support, and helped Democratic candidates in 1876 and 1880. A decline in agricultural production in 1884 and a depression in the early 1890s contributed to Democrat Grover Cleveland's two non-successive elections in 1884 and 1892. And dissatisfaction by Midwest farmers, evident throughout the 1880s, and later by farmers in the South and the West, gave the Democrats an issue on which to stand. The Populists, carrying the banner of agricultural America as a third party, played much the same role as had the abolitionists half a century earlier.

The election of 1896 stands as a clear dividing point. The Democrats had suffered huge losses in the midterm election of 1894, as a reaction to the depression of 1893 during Cleveland's second term. The standard-bearer for the Democrats, the charismatic William Jennings Bryan, attacked big business and took up the cause of rural America, calling for easier credit and adoption of a silver standard. No one would deny the power of Bryan's rhetoric, but he defined for his party a losing coalition.

> The great cities rest upon our broad and fertile prairies. Burn down your cities and leave our farms, and your cities will spring up again as if by magic; but destroy our farms and the grass will grow in the streets of every city in the country.... You shall not crucify mankind upon a cross of gold.
>
> William Jennings Bryan's "Cross of Gold" speech
> Democratic National Convention, July 1896

The 1896 election realigned the electorate. The Republicans became the party of the cities, of workers and industrialists; the Democrats remained dominant in the South and border states, but still a minority party. The only two presidential elections that the Republicans lost over the next nine were those won by Woodrow Wilson, in 1912 because the Republican party was split by the third party candidacy of former president, Theodore Roosevelt, and in 1916 when Wilson barely won reelection. Republican control of Congress followed the pattern of presidential voting, as few in the electorate split their tickets at this time.

The electoral coalitions that remained stable through the first quarter of the twentieth century were shattered by the Great Depression of 1929 and the two parties' responses to that crisis. Once again, the party labels remained the same, the Democrats and the Republicans, but former Republicans became ardent Democrats and those who had felt equally strongly about the Democratic party switched to become Republicans. Republican Herbert Hoover, president during the onset of the Depression, argued for staying the course. His Democratic challenger in 1932, New York governor Franklin Delano Roosevelt, argued for change during the campaign and chose a different course once in office.

Roosevelt's advisors followed Keynesian economic doctrine and advocated policies that emphasized government intervention in the economy and deficit spending to stimulate economic growth—a New Deal for America. The government became the employer of last resort, the provider for those who were without the necessities of life, the benevolent force in the lives of those in need. Economists can debate whether Roosevelt's policies pulled the nation out of the Depression—or whether the economic stimulus necessitated by the lead up to World War II had that effect—but none can deny that the public perception of his policies changed electoral politics for decades to come.

The Democrats maintained their dominance in the South largely for cultural reasons from the Civil War. But Roosevelt's New Deal coalition added the support of labor union members and of small farmers, of minorities and of ethnic Americans, of the poor and of those fighting for equal rights. The Republicans became the party of big business and of the affluent. Roosevelt led the nation into World War II, and he gained popularity as the wartime leader. He broke the precedent set by George Washington that presidents should serve only two terms, winning a third term in 1940 and a fourth in 1944, before dying in office in April 1945. The Democrats controlled the Congress during his tenure in office and, with one minor exception, maintained that control into the last decade of the century.

The New Deal coalition dominated American politics into the 1960s; one cataclysmic event did not shatter it, but rather it was broken gradually as different issues confronted the electorate and citizens' memories of the events that led to their party loyalties or to their parents' loyalties dimmed. In the 1960s Republican presidential candidate Barry Goldwater made the first inroads into Democratic dominance in the South. Richard Nixon followed a southern strategy of appealing to voters whose loyalty to the Democratic party was based more on tradition than on policy preferences. Since that time, the South has moved more and more toward the Republicans, not only for presidential elections but also for state and local offices.

The Vietnam War also brought traditional party loyalties into question. Much of the opposition to that war came from Democrats; many traditional blue-collar Democrats felt that opposing a war while troops were in harm's way was unpatriotic; they moved to the Republican party in protest. Others left the Democrats because they felt the party had become isolationist, not willing to stand up to the rest of the world.

On domestic issues the Democrats came to be associated with what some viewed as extreme social positions. During the 1972

presidential campaign, the Democrats were dubbed the party of "amnesty [for draft evaders], acid, and abortion." The allegiance of more socially conservative Democrats was tested. The presidency of Ronald Reagan stretched traditional loyalties further. Reagan was a charismatic leader with a clearly stated philosophy. He favored a strong defense and lower taxes, cutting welfare programs and supporting traditional social values. Leaders of more conservative, but traditionally Democratic unions joined his supporters. Reagan Democrats, traditional Democrats who voted for President Reagan and the Republicans in the 1980s, were an important part of his winning coalition.

As the twentieth century drew to a close, the rise of conservative Christians as a political force further complicated analysis of

5. Ronald Reagan accepts the presidential nomination at the Republican National Convention in Dallas, Texas, on August 23, 1984. Describing a partisan view of the differences between the Republicans and Democrats, he said, "The choices this year are ... between two fundamentally different ways of governing—their government of pessimism, fear, and limits, or ours of hope, confidence, and growth."

political coalitions. Many conservative Christians who should have favored the Democrats for economic reasons voted Republican. Partisan politics became increasingly bitter, with compromise positions to solve pressing national problems difficult to forge. The partisan balance, as exemplified by the closeness of the Bush-Gore presidential election in 2000 and the party divisions in each house of Congress, is precarious. It is clear where the two parties stand on some of the issues. However, more policy issues seem to overlap. Social issues divide the electorate in one way; economic issues, in another; international issues, in perhaps a third. Politicians, seeing this, emphasize extreme positions on wedge issues that further divide the country. The Republican party has had particular difficulty, as many economic conservatives are uncomfortable with the extremely conservative social stands taken by some seeking to carry the party banner.

From this review it is clear that at various times in American history the division between the parties has directly reflected a policy divide in the nation; at other times this correlation has been less clear. As the national government has become involved in more areas of citizens' lives, and as those lives themselves have become increasingly complex and more involved in a global community, the extent to which partisan differences can reflect the often subtle and internally conflicted citizens' views on the issues becomes more difficult.

In the early years, the parties were instruments of political leaders seeking a following in the country. But they evolved into institutions that play a major role in the electoral process, without which American politics is unimaginable. Another important part of party history, then, is a story of institutional development.

American political parties as institutions

The development of parties as institutions begins in earnest with the democratizing reforms of the Jacksonian period (1829–37).

Popular participation in the electoral process was the centerpiece of Jacksonian democracy, drawing the lesson from John Quincy Adams's winning the White House after losing the popular vote. Rejecting the old method of nomination by congressional caucus, caricatured as King Caucus, prior to the 1832 election, parties began to hold conventions, with delegates coming from around the nation to select presidential candidates. By the 1830s the norm was for states to choose presidential electors by popular elections, not by balloting within the state legislature. In order to connect representatives in Washington to their constituents, states moved to district, rather than at-large, elections of U.S. representatives, a practice written into law in the Census Act of 1840. Governors, who had often been selected by state legislatures in the early days, came to be popularly elected, and citizens were asked to vote on many state and local officials.

As a result political parties began to organize at the local level in order to fill ballot slots, to support candidates, and to get out the vote. By the 1840s both parties had complex, decentralized organizations. In 1848 the Democrats formed a national committee (and the Republicans followed suit less than a decade later); the national committees, however, were clearly less powerful than their state and local counterparts. Nonetheless, by mid-century formal organizations from the local to the national level were in place in both major political parties, and they have remained so since.

As the franchise spread to a larger portion of the citizenry, the parties adopted campaign techniques to reach the voters. Candidates were often old generals who recalled their military exploits with catchy slogans—Jackson himself, the hero of the Battle of New Orleans in the War of 1812, was "Old Hickory"; "Tippecanoe and Tyler Too" were William Henry Harrison, the victor of the Battle of Tippecanoe against a group of American Indians, and his running mate John Tyler; "Old Rough and Ready" was war hero Zachary Taylor, elected president in 1848.

Politicians learned to use inflammatory rhetoric to excite the voters; parties ran torchlight parades to stoke the competitive fires of their followers. Getting out the vote meant getting the common man to the polls, and then, as now, the average voter was not stirred by philosophical debates; the spoils system, with the spoils in terms of postelection employment going to supporters of the winning candidate, and the excitement of campaign events were the stuff of politics at mid-century.

The latter half of the nineteenth century is known as the "gilded age of parties." Party competition was incredibly intense. As a result parties put a premium on organizing to get their supporters to the polls, particularly in marginal districts; they had to be disciplined, organized, and energetic.

Party machines, structured hierarchies dominated by political bosses, with workers organized down to the most local level, the voting precinct, came into existence during this period. Party workers' and voters' loyalty to the machine was cemented by material incentives, tangible rewards that were given when elections were won and, by implication, would be removed if the elections were lost. Party workers often held lucrative patronage jobs—and they worked hard for the machine to keep those jobs. An important part of their task was to recruit new loyalists, and new immigrants were tempting targets. The party in power provided new citizens with all forms of aid—jobs, lodging, the extra treats at Thanksgiving and Christmas, and, perhaps most important to new arrivals, socialization into their new community. In return, the machine received votes—and loyalty.

The party machines that dominated urban areas at the end of the nineteenth century were parties of patronage, not principle. Their job was to win elections; they recruited candidates for local office, but they cared more about the jobs those officials could hand out than the policies they passed. Most patronage jobs were controlled by local or county government.

At the state level, party machines, particularly Republican party machines, were run differently. In those cases the fuel was money, provided by business interests, more than jobs and aid for new voters. State machines were often run by U.S. senators, because at this time U.S. senators were chosen by state legislatures. The business interest supported the boss, who was elected by the state legislature and went to Washington to protect the interests of those who supported his organization. The fuel that ran the machine was different, but the material nature of the incentives for loyalty was the same.

One important mechanism of party control was control over the nominating process. Party bosses decided who the nominees would be. They then printed and distributed the ballots, so that they controlled the fate of those nominees. The workings of the parties were out of sight and well beyond the control of the average citizen.

Party machines reached their peak at the turn of the century. Their decline began with reforms of the early twentieth century and proceeded, at different paces in different areas but inevitably, from then on. The invention and then spread of the direct primary election took control of nominations out of the hands of party leaders. The civil service system removed many patronage jobs from party control. The Seventeenth Amendment to the U.S. Constitution, passed in 1913, required direct election of U.S. senators, taking one of the last powers away from state party machines. Welfare reforms passed as part of the New Deal in response to the Great Depression meant that the federal government, not the parties, was the source of aid for needy citizens—and loyalty was transferred accordingly. While vestiges of party machines could be found in certain urban centers well past mid-century, Mayor Richard J. Daley's Cook County machine in Chicago standing as a prime example, those last dominating party organizations were the exception, not the rule.

6. President Lyndon Johnson (right) pays homage to Chicago's longtime political boss, Mayor Richard Daley.

Parties, however, did not disappear. If parties as campaign organizations were on the wane, parties as a means to organize the government and as a symbol to which citizens showed loyalty remained strong. In the early twentieth century both parties, in both houses of Congress, began to elect formal leaders, whether the party held majority or minority status. Party members in legislatures were expected to follow their leaders. The party of the president was expected to support that president's legislative program. Newly elected presidents routinely chose members of their own party to fill cabinet and subcabinet jobs.

Voters might have lost material incentives to support one party or the other, but their loyalty remained. The partisan division during the New Deal was extremely deep. President Roosevelt was viewed as a savior by Democrats; he was viewed as a demon by Republicans. Voter loyalty to party transcended issue and, except for in the case of charismatic leaders like General Dwight D. Eisenhower, when he ran for president in 1952,

personality. Party organizations remained in existence, but their power was gone.

However, to paraphrase Mark Twain, rumors of the death of political parties have been greatly exaggerated. Not only has the two-party system not died, but the Democratic and Republican parties persist and continue to dominate. Unlike in the early eighteenth century, when the Federalists disappeared and two-party competition ended for a while, that did not happen in the mid-twentieth century because each party now exists as an organization, and organizations adapt to maintain their existence; they do not fold up their tents and sulk away.

The adaptation by political parties involved responding to a situation in which the campaign tools they used were no longer as relevant, in which loyalty was not to the organization per se, in which ticket-splitting, voting for Democrats for some offices and Republicans for others, became routine, and in which candidates ran campaigns on their own, not in lockstep alliance with other members of their parties. Put simply, parties adapted to a new situation by taking on a role that candidates needed to have filled. For new campaign technologies—first radio, then television, then ever more sophisticated use of computers for polling and direct voter contact—money was needed. Parties took on the role of raising money for candidates. They did this at the national level, through the national committees and the four separate committees charged with overseeing congressional and senatorial campaigns, to so-called Hill committees (the Democratic Congressional Campaign Committee, the Democratic Senatorial Campaign Committee, the National Republican Congressional Committee, and the National Republican Senatorial Committee); they passed money from the national level down to the state levels; they provided services, such as polling and opposition research, for candidates who could not afford to do so. They served as a go-between, easing contact for candidates in their party with

representatives of interest groups likely to support them and with wealthy individual donors. The parties have essentially become service organizations for their candidates for office; but in that role they play a very important part of national campaigns.

The political historian Joel Silbey divides the history of American parties into four eras, according to how central the role of parties has been to American life. The early period, up to the Jackson presidency, is described as a *preparty period*. The period from then through the gilded age of parties is called the *party period*. The period in which party's role is seen to be declining is a *postparty period*; the current era he characterizes as a *nonparty period*. Perhaps that is so, in terms of the centrality of party to American life, but parties—particularly as campaign organizations and as means to organize the government—remain vibrant and active today. They do not play the role they once did, but they have adapted and found a new role. If one does not understand that role, one cannot understand modern American elections.

The system in which American political parties function

To this point we have discussed how the American parties have reflected policy divisions within the electorate, and the development and adaptation of parties as political institutions. But institutions exist—and policy is developed—within a broader political system. Changes in that system lead inevitably to changes in the functioning of institutions and just as inevitably to alterations in the policy arena. We will briefly consider three areas in which important changes have taken place—the electorate, what offices are contested under what rules, and what techniques are used to contest elections—looking in each case at the implications for political parties and the electoral process.

Expansion of the electorate

At the time of the founding, in most states voting was the exclusive prerogative of white, male property owners. Today, universal suffrage is the rule, with debate over how to raise turnout, to convince those eligible to vote to exercise the franchise. The history of expansion of the electorate has progressed in four phases.

The first step was removal of the property-owning requirement, which was eliminated on a state-by-state basis, usually to be replaced with a requirement that voters be taxpayers. The taxpayer requirement persisted, in the form of a poll tax, a tax levied as a citizen exercised the right to vote, until it too was eliminated—for federal offices by the Twenty-fourth Amendment to the Constitution (ratified in 1964) and for all elections by the Supreme Court in the case of *Harper v. Virginia State Board of Elections* 383 U.S. 663 (1966).

Next came the extension of suffrage to blacks, a process that took more than a century to complete. After the Civil War, the Fifteenth Amendment, ratified in 1870, stated that no citizen could be denied the right to vote based on "race, color, or previous condition of servitude." However, legislatures in former slaveholding states adopted ingenious means of keeping the newly enfranchised former slaves from voting. The so-called Jim Crow laws included literacy tests, tests on interpreting the Constitution, "whites only" primaries (that defined the parties as private associations open only to whites), residency requirements, and poll taxes. Southern communities often placed voting booths far from areas in which former slaves resided and opened them only for limited hours. These legal restrictions were supplemented with illegal means—intimidation and physical abuse. The result was that in 1960, fewer than 15 percent of the African American citizens living in Alabama, Mississippi, and South Carolina were registered to vote; only about 30 percent of the African Americans living throughout the South were registered in that year. The Voting Rights Act of 1965 addressed the inequality of political rights that resulted from these

practices. That act specified that the determination that less than 50 percent of a racial minority was registered to vote in any county constituted prima facie evidence of discrimination, and federal registrars would replace local officials to guarantee that racial minorities were given equal treatment with regard to voting. The Voting Rights Act was one of the most important products of the Civil Rights movement of the 1960s. By the decade's end, the percentage of African Americans registered to vote had more than doubled throughout the region and had grown more than fourfold in the states with the lowest percentage registered earlier. While African American voting turnout still trails the national average, the most significant legal barriers to voting have been removed.

The third stage in the expansion of the franchise was extending the vote to women. The epic battles waged by women suffragists, from the Seneca Falls convention issuing its Declaration of Sentiments regarding woman rights in 1848 through ratification of the

7. A woman suffrage procession makes its way through the streets of Washington, DC, on March 3, 1913. The expansion of the franchise had the potential to double the size of the electorate.

Woman Suffrage Amendment to the Constitution, the Nineteenth Amendment ratified in 1920, rightly deserve the volumes dedicated to them. Fighting simultaneously on a state-by-state basis and on the national stage, the suffragists sought to gain an equal share of power, not just from those holding it but from those with whom they shared a home and bed. That they succeeded is testament to the strength and skill of their leaders, to their perseverance, and to the triumph of people of principle over people of power.

These three stages of expansion of the electorate all made significant difference in the electoral process in the United States. In the early days of the republic, only about one in thirty could vote; politics was an avocation of the elite. There was little need to consider the views of the average man. But extending the franchise to all taxpayers fundamentally changed the game; as the players changed, those seeking election had to adopt new strategies or, as in the case of the Federalists, disappear.

Strom Thurmond

Strom Thurmond made his career in South Carolina as a race-baiter, as a segregationist politician who stood up for the way of life that some southerners yearned for. In 1948 he ran for president as a States' Rights, pro-segregationist candidate. By the 1980s, however, Thurmond, who became a Republican in the 1960s, because Lyndon Johnson was too strong on civil rights, had an African American receptionist in his Senate office. No longer could those in power in the South ignore their African American constituents. In 2015 his son, South Carolina state senator Paul Thurmond, was one of the leaders of the effort to remove the Confederate battle flag from the state capitol grounds, after the murder of nine African Americans attending a Charleston AME church Bible study session.

Extension of the vote to African Americans was a statement of principle in the first place, but, the theoretical right to vote was converted into actual voting power in the 1960s. Especially in the South, large segments of the population whose views and desires had been safely ignored by elected politicians, because the politicians knew that African Americans did not vote, now became relevant.

When women received the right to vote, on a state-by-state basis near the end of the nineteenth century and nationally in 1920, the eligible electorate doubled. Those in power—party leaders, union leaders, the liquor industry, the Catholic Church, business leaders—all opposed women voting, because they feared that policies on which their power depended would be reversed overnight. That did not happen, but the nature of politics did change, with parties adopting platform planks appealing to women and adapting campaign techniques and strategies accordingly. At various times in the twentieth century women came together on issues of special concern to them; at times they voted significantly differently from their male counterparts. But, by and large, women's voting behavior did not differ significantly from that of men.

The fourth and last stage in the expansion of the franchise occurred when the voting age was lowered from twenty-one in most states to eighteen. President Eisenhower, who as supreme commander of the Allied Expeditionary Force in Europe during World War II, had sent hundreds of thousands of young men into harm's way, understood the contradiction inherent in a law that kept those between eighteen and twenty-one from voting, while they could be drafted. He asked Congress to lower the voting age to eighteen in his 1955 State of the Union Address and insisted on Alaska and Hawaii having lower voting ages in order to join the Union.

But it was not until 1971, during the Vietnam War, that the issue reached a national crescendo, leading to the passage of the Twenty-sixth Amendment to the Constitution, lowering the

minimum voting age to eighteen. While some feared and others hoped that the newly enfranchised youth would vote as a liberal bloc, this prediction has never been realized. Young voters participate at much lower rates than their older peers; they do not differ significantly in how they vote from older voters with similar racial, social, and economic backgrounds.

Offices contested in American elections

If expansion of the franchise altered participation, changes in the contested offices altered the objective of the electoral process itself. Again, a progression can be noted, and the result has clear implications for the electoral process itself.

The progression is seen in an increase in the number of elections for office put before citizens. One can see the pattern without describing the steps in great detail. At the time of the founding, the president, U.S. senators, and most governors were elected with little or no popular participation. The president was elected indirectly, by the Electoral College, and few of the electors were chosen in popular elections; governors were often elected by state legislatures; U.S. senators were selected by state legislatures; and many local officials were appointed.

All of that has changed. While the Electoral College still elects the president, electors are now popularly chosen in every state, and there is considerable agitation toward eliminating the Electoral College altogether. All state governors are popularly elected. Since the passage of the Seventeenth Amendment in 1913, U.S. senators have been popularly elected. And now judges are elected in many states. Local officials continue to be elected in numbers beyond those in any other democracy. While the number of elected officials has increased, the number of political appointees these officials can name to office has decreased radically.

As a result, electoral politics is much less about the spoils of office and more about appealing to the electorate in other ways.

Presidents and statewide officeholders portray a public image that appeals to the electorate. That trend can be seen as far back as the mid-nineteenth century, when parties nominated war heroes to whom the electorate could relate. The trend is more obvious in the age of television and mass communications. Could someone who looked like Lincoln be elected in the modern era? Other officeholders, those in less visible offices, have developed other techniques to reach the voters. Congressmen and state legislators spend a good deal of their own and their staff's time on constituent service, looking out for the needs of individuals and of communities as they relate to their government. All of these changes have clear and quite obvious effects on the electoral process.

Campaign techniques

Howard Dean's unsuccessful campaign for the Democratic nomination in 2004 demonstrates the third systemic change, change in campaign techniques. He relied on the Internet to reach voters, to organize his campaign and to raise money, using technology in ways never tried before, but in a sense his campaign was only the latest in a long series using technological innovations in a political context.

One hundred years ago politicians reached citizens on a one-on-one basis. Personal contact was the only possible means of contact, whether by mail or face-to-face. Politicians did not use radio as a means to communicate or as a campaign technique until the presidency of Franklin Delano Roosevelt.

Since that time we have seen three separate technological revolutions in campaigning. First, candidates now communicate differently with the electorate. Radio has been replaced by television as the principal means of communication with potential voters. Broadcasting over television has been supplemented by "narrowcasting," buying advertisements on cable outlets that appeal to particular subsets of the population and designing messages accordingly. Internet appeals and social

media connections further refine the ways in which candidates communicate their messages to prospective voters and raise funds.

Second, candidates find out information about the electorate in increasingly sophisticated ways. Computer technology revolutionized the polling industry. Whereas once only national campaigns or the most expensive statewide campaigns could afford public opinion polling, and a benchmark poll at the beginning of a campaign and one or two subsequent polls was considered state-of-the-art research, now national and even statewide campaigns poll continuously. They use rolling samples to gauge changing public views on a day-to-day or event-to-event basis. Polling is commonplace in many local elections. Whereas once pollsters were told to work their craft, provide their information to campaign strategists, and stand aside, now they are campaign strategists, working closely (often in the same firm) with media consultants, direct mail consultants, fund-raisers, and the inner circle of a candidate's campaign. Information that is gathered is more sophisticated, more timely, and clearly more central to defining campaign messages.

Third, campaigns gather and analyze data with increased sophistication. Faster and cheaper computer technology now allows campaigns to gather, store, and analyze data—on supporters, on volunteers, on donors, on issues, on opponents—in much more sophisticated ways. Fund-raising has changed dramatically, because campaigns can target appeals with precision. Campaign organizing can be done with increased sophistication, with much of the communication handled instantly over the Internet. Candidate speeches and debate preparation can be more clearly tailored to audiences, can reference government programs more precisely, and can counter opponents' claims more swiftly, all because of computerized data analysis.

Even with these changes, politics remains as much art as science. Recall again the presidential primary campaign of Howard Dean in 2004. Dean, former governor of the small state of Vermont,

harnessed the Internet as no candidate had before. He took a technique pioneered four years earlier by Republican John McCain and used the Internet to raise vast sums of money; none of the other candidates understood the power of this tool until the Dean campaign demonstrated it. He used Internet communications to build a vast army of volunteers, all connected instantaneously with the campaign messages. He targeted the voters to whom he appealed in a precise and sophisticated way. Yet, he lost. He lost, in part to be sure, because he lost his cool one night in Iowa—and the very same people who were listening so intently to his message saw a different side of the man they had supported.

He lost more fundamentally because others in the contest understood the game as well—and they applied their art. In 2008, Barack Obama's campaign applied those lessons—and captured the desire of the nation for change—using the new techniques with their own artful touch. In 2012, the Romney campaign applied the 2008 Obama techniques, but Obama went further and understood voters' desires better. Campaigns learn techniques and quickly catch up; but the art of reaching a broad base of the electorate is more difficult to learn.

Summary

This brief history of American political parties is instructive for understanding the electoral process today. Parties have changed throughout this nation's history. The parties have changed as institutions; the issues of the day have defined the appeals that they have made to the electorate; the electorate itself has changed, as have the offices that are contested; and the ways in which appeals are made have changed as the technology important to campaigning has advanced.

But at the same time, the electoral process has not changed. It is still about contesting for public support of candidates based on

what the voters think those candidates have done and are likely to do in the future. It is still about winners and losers—for in the American system, close does not count. And it is still about organizing, understanding the rules and the voters and how one can appeal to the voters most efficiently under the rules in play.

Chapter 3

Party organizations: What do they look like? What do they do?

According to his eulogist, longtime New York state senator George Washington Plunkitt, one of the leaders of New York's Tammany Hall political machine at the turn of the twentieth century, "understood that in politics honesty doesn't matter, efficiency doesn't matter, progressive vision doesn't matter. What does matter is the chance for a better job, a better price of wheat, better business conditions." At its height the machine controlled more than 12,000 jobs, with an annual payroll of over $12 million, more than leading iron and steel corporations of the time.

During the "gilded age of parties," more than a century ago, party organizations, often well-oiled political party machines, did the business of governing. They recruited the candidates and set the governing agendas; they socialized the citizens and brought them to the polls; they populated the civil service and provided the link between citizens and their government. Party bosses were legendary for their power and their influence—and often for their corruption. As Plunkitt said, defending his personal gains, "I seen my chances and I took 'em." That was how the business of politics was run.

Even in the first half of the twentieth century, in city after city urban bosses controlled access to politics. James Michael Curley

was the boss of Boston, Massachusetts, for most of the first half of the century. The Pendergast machine in Kansas City, Missouri, came to power in the second decade of the twentieth century and remained powerful enough to claim credit for placing Harry Truman in the Senate and eventually in the White House. The Crump machine in Memphis, Tennessee, dominated that city's politics until after World War II. The same can be said of Frank Hague's machine in Jersey City, New Jersey. William J. Green's machine in Philadelphia, David Lawrence's in Pittsburgh, and Richard J. Daley's in Chicago all were still important enough in 1960 to contribute importantly to John F. Kennedy's nomination for the presidency.

Party organizations were clearly structured at that time. They were hierarchical organizations with material incentives linking the populace to precinct captains and district leaders and even greater material incentives linking those leaders to the hierarchy in city halls and county court houses. The material incentives of jobs and additional assistance of food and clothing for the immigrants flooding American cities were supplemented with solidary incentives, a feeling of kinship, help for the newly arrived as they made their way in a strange land, a place to gather and to mix and mingle with like-minded people.

These organizations were dominated by powerful leaders who understood that their power was a direct function of those beholden to them remaining in office. To say that rules were bent to achieve this end is an understatement. And the bosses were not shy about their goals and their motives. Tom Pendergast put it simply, in his one rule of politics: "The important thing is to get the votes—no matter what." Frank Hague expressed his view on politics somewhat differently: "I am the law....I decide; I do; ME!" The bosses got the job done; they were loyally followed by the voters who benefited from their largesse; their means were often ignored.

The story of the demise of the machines is a complex one—involving democratic reformers, the government assuming many of the responsibilities for social welfare that parties once performed, exposure of corruption, and other factors that varied by locale. By the last quarter of the twentieth century only the palest shadows of these once powerful organizations remained.

In the twenty-first century, these machines seem a relic from a bygone era, but party organization persists. Whereas once party organization built from the most local level, through counties and states to the national level, today the power in the organization flows largely from the national level down. Whereas once parties controlled the nominating process and candidates were creatures of the parties, today candidates establish their own organizations to run in primaries and the political party organizations exist largely to serve the needs of those candidates who are nominated or who, once elected, are seeking reelection. Whereas once the work of parties depended on personal connections and personal contact with the voters, today the work of political parties focuses on providing money and the means for electronic communications.

American political parties do not resemble the programmatic parties typically found in Western democracies. The party organizations and their leaders play virtually no role in shaping policy agendas. In fact, one could argue that American parties, for at least the last half century, have been in search of a role. However, organizations continue to exist at the local, county, state, and national level; in recent election cycles party organizations, all but unknown to the voting public, have played critical roles in various aspects of the electoral process, from nominations through the general elections.

The national political party organizations

Perhaps the best way to begin a discussion of party organizations in the United States is to ask a simple question: Can you name the chair of the Democratic National Committee (DNC) or of the Republican National Committee (RNC)? Non-American readers might claim that the question is unfair, that only Americans would know such information. American readers are scratching their heads, unsure exactly who holds these positions, much less what they do.

The national party chairs

Table 3.1 lists the holders of the top positions in the national party organizations since 2005. Not exactly a list of household names. In fact, only the name of Howard Dean, who ran a very visible, though unsuccessful campaign for the 2004 Democratic presidential nomination, is familiar to most citizens, even those who follow politics closely. The contrast between Dean and his Republican counterpart, Ken Mehlman, is instructive.

Mehlman's path to the chairmanship of the Republican National Committee is quite typical. First, he was the choice of the successful Republican candidate for president, George W. Bush. Incumbent presidents dominate their party's national committee and typically are very influential in choosing its head. Second, Mehlman came to his post through a series of political jobs. In 2000 he was the field director for Bush's presidential campaign; when Bush was successful, Mehlman, who had begun his political career working for a series of Texas Republicans in the House of Representatives, went to the White House as Director of Political Affairs. He left that job to assume the position as campaign manager for the Bush-Cheney reelection campaign. Mehlman is a political operative, closely tied to the incumbent president, expert in running campaigns, not in setting policy. Although he was officially elected by the members of the Republican National Committee, he was in fact chosen by his boss, George W. Bush.

Table 3.1 Democratic and republican national committee chairs

Democratic National Committee chairs

Howard Dean, 2005–2009
Former governor of Vermont; unsuccessful candidate for party's presidential nomination

Tim Kaine, 2009–2011
Former governor of Virginia

Debbie Wasserman Schultz, 2011–present
U.S Representative for Florida's Twenty-Third Congressional District

Republican National Committee chairs

Ken Mehlman, 2005–2007
Campaign manager for Bush–Cheney '04

Mel Martinez, 2007
Lobbyist and former U.S. senator from Florida

Mike Duncan, 2007–2009
Served as general counsel of the RNC

Michael Steele, 2009–2011
Former lieutenant governor of Maryland

Reince Priebus, 2011–present
Former chairman of the Wisconsin Republican Party

By way of contrast, political observers were shocked when Howard Dean announced his interest in running the Democratic National Committee. Dean made his reputation as a political iconoclast. When he began his campaign for the Democratic presidential nomination, few observers gave him any chance. He was an unknown governor of a small state, an outsider intent on challenging the status quo and the party establishment. He took what some deemed to be extreme positions on the issues of the day; he did not seek endorsements from the party leaders; he developed

an innovative but untried campaign strategy based largely on the Internet. Dean succeeded beyond anyone's expectations. Even though he did not win the nomination, he changed the ways funds were raised and campaigns were run, energized the left wing of his party that had grown disenchanted with mainstream party candidates, and altered the issue agenda.

Then he decided to take over the party organization. His candidacy caused concern among party centrists who feared that his approach would alienate the political center, necessary for national victories. Dean did little to allay these fears. In an email to his supporters announcing his candidacy, he said simply, "Our party must speak plainly and our agenda must clearly reflect the socially progressive, fiscally responsible values that bring our party—and the vast majority of Americans—together." Party leaders worried about the "speak plainly" aspect of that statement and that he would be too progressive on social issues for a national audience.

But they also realized that the Democrats had lost two straight presidential elections with mainstream, establishment candidates running campaigns that paled in comparison to the Republican's effort, that their party had not controlled the Congress in a decade, that the party was losing strength at the state and local levels, and that Dean had demonstrated real strengths in technological innovation, in fund-raising, and in organizing. In the end, many swallowed their fears, and Dean was elected by the Democratic National Committee over a strong field of traditional political operatives.

And how did these two leaders differ in their styles? Mehlman performed as a fairly typical party chair. As President Bush's popularity plummeted in the winter of 2005–6—in the wake of difficult times in Iraq, the perceived failure of the federal government response to Hurricane Katrina, scandals involving members of the administration, presidentially authorized wiretaps of questionable legality by the National Security Administration,

and perceived cronyism in some appointments—Mehlman was the president's staunchest defender. He was at the front line of taking media questions about each situation—and responded with the most positive spin possible.

Dean played a different role. He traveled into strongly Republican areas and carried his message of a Democratic party standing firmly on issues of principle. While he did not back away from his mission, he was not always welcomed by local Democrats; in the South in particular, local Democrats appreciated that Dean as the DNC chair cared about their state, but many believed that his message was wrong for their constituents. A number of elected officials were notably absent from his appearances.

Dean's plain speaking did not abate. At one point Dean characterized the Republican Party as "pretty much a white, Christian Party." His comment was met with disdain by elected party leaders. Connecticut senator Joe Lieberman said, "It was divisive and wrong and I hope he apologizes for it." Delaware senator Joseph Biden's reaction to Dean's language was similar: "He doesn't speak for me with that kind of rhetoric. And I don't think he speaks for the majority of Democrats."

National party organization staffs

To this point, we have pointed to the role of DNC and RNC chairs, but we have talked little about the committees they head. Each party's national committee is comprised of members chosen by party organizations in each state and territory of the nation. While the committees hold the formal power in the parties, chairs play a much more visible role and much of the work is done by the staffs. The committee staffs, working out of large, permanent party headquarters in the shadow of the U.S. Capitol, raise money, plan strategy, devise tactics, do research, provide resources, and ready the party and its candidates for each campaign cycle. One of the most important functions of the national committee staffs is to

monitor how campaigns are running throughout the nation, which campaigns are clearly won and which lost, which are hotly contested, which candidates need financial help, and the like. Then they funnel resources accordingly.

Table 3.2 presents some interesting comparisons. The states with approximately the same populations are paired. In each case, the two national committees have transferred significantly more to the competitive state than to the noncompetitive state. To put the party efforts in starkest terms, the two national parties transferred nearly identical sums of money to the Colorado state committees as they did to those in California. Colorado, which was a competitive state in 2012, has a population approximately one-tenth that of California, which saw little competition in that election.

The Democratic and Republican National Committees

The Democratic National Committee (DNC) is comprised of 440 members; there are nine officers (the chair, five vice chairs, secretary, treasurer, national finance chair); each geographic jurisdiction is represented by its chair and the highest ranking officer of the opposite sex; 200 additional members are apportioned among the states according to population; elected Democratic officials from the national to the local level and party constituencies (e.g., college Democrats) are represented by a total of 27 members; the chair can appoint up to 50 at-large members to represent groups thought to be important to the party but underrepresented on the DNC (e.g., ethnic or racial minorities or unions).

The Republican National Committee (RNC) is a much simpler body. It consists of the chair and one committeeman and one committeewoman from each state and territory. Officers are the chair, a co-chair of the opposite sex, and four male and four female vice chairs, chosen on a regional basis.

Table 3.2 Transfers from national committees to state committees, 2011–2012

State	RNC	DNC
Arkansas	$158,241	$352,214
Kansas	$20,544	$321,852
Colorado	$8,161,056	$8,161,056
Maryland	$62,953	$421, 299
Florida	$17,672,435	$16,545,511
Texas	$256,058	$1,091,614
Illinois	$1,568,819	$1,917,445
Ohio	$16,236,531	$16,236,531
Iowa	$4,689,896	$7,034,845
Kansas	$20,544	$321,852
Maine	$434,403	$550,332
Rhode Island	$448,680	$263,510
Massachusetts	$6,188,307	$2,174,270
Washington	$88,808	$1,391,326

The chairs and the staffs of the national committees work closely with their counterparts at the four so-called Hill committees, each housed in national party headquarters. The National Republican Congressional Committee (NRCC), the National Republican Senatorial Committee (NRSC), the Democratic Congressional Campaign Committee (DCCC), and the Democratic Senatorial Campaign Committee (DSCC) have become central players in the biennial campaigns for control of the houses of Congress. Each of the Hill committees is chaired by an incumbent member of Congress, who, by virtue of this position, is a member of his or her

party's leadership in the chamber. Their job is simple: to protect seats held by incumbents and to win open seats and those of vulnerable members of the other party.

The Hill committees have been in existence for a long time—the House committees since just after the Civil War and the Senate committees shortly after the Seventeenth Amendment, calling for popular election of U.S. senators, was ratified in 1913. But they have played minor roles for much of their history, merely helping incumbents to raise money. In the last two decades, however, their role has increased dramatically. Not only do they raise money for candidates, but they play critical roles in setting national campaign priorities.

The prominence of the Hill committees was abundantly clear in the 2006 congressional election cycles. In 2004 fewer than twenty congressional districts were thought to be in play. The concept of a district "in play" is a relatively new one. While incumbents have been seen to have an electoral advantage for some time, only recently have political operatives conceded large numbers of districts well in advance of the election (often more than a year in advance) and concentrated their efforts on relatively few. The NRCC and the DCCC, each using their own criteria, seek to limit the number of districts in which they are active to those in which the outcome is seriously in doubt; then they concentrate their efforts in those districts. The two political organizations—and the political analysts who monitor congressional races, such as the *Cook Political Report* and the *Rothenberg and Gonzales Political Report*—have been remarkably consistent and accurate in predicting which races will be close.

Early in the 2006 electoral cycle, both parties and the nonpartisan analysts were looking at approximately the same number of seats. Since the Democrats needed to pick up fifteen seats to regain control of the House of Representatives, most thought their chances slim. But, the political winds shifted in the Democrats' direction. By the

fall of 2005, DCCC chair Rahm Emanuel (D-IL) was successfully recruiting strong Democratic challengers for approximately fifty seats, in all of the open seats and some held by Republicans suddenly thought to be vulnerable. NRCC chair Tom Reynolds (R-NY), while claiming that the political map still favored his party, understood that his task was to defend vulnerable incumbents in what was an expanding number of seats. As the number of seats in play expanded, the accuracy of the party perceptions of the political lay of the land became more critical. In all campaigns resources are scarce; how they are allocated often marks the difference between victory and defeat.

The 2006 cycle also led to the first public rift between a national chair and the chairs of the Hill committees. DNC chair Dean continued to explore means to show the Democratic flag in heavily Republican areas, spending time and money in so doing. DCCC chair Emanuel and his Senate counterpart, New York senator Charles Schumer, argued that money should be concentrated in winnable seats. In the year before the election, the difference on strategy led to a rift that became heated and public, with Dean and Emanuel not even speaking to each other. The 2006 scenario provides a clear indication how the roles and responsibilities of different party actors lead to different responses to political situations.

Electoral roles of the national committees' staff

What role do the parties play in the election campaigns they target? When party organizations dominated the American political scene, the key to their power was to have officeholders loyal to the organization in place; and the key to that was control of the nominating process. In part the decline of parties can be traced to losing control of the nominating process as a result of direct primary elections.

In twenty-first-century politics, however, the key to winning elections is often in finding a strong candidate to run. Many incumbents win reelection because their opponents are either

weak or nonexistent (i.e., incumbents run without any major party opposition). A key role for parties today is to recruit strong candidates to run in open seats and to oppose incumbents in the other party. Party leaders such as Emanuel can do this only if they can convince the potential candidate that the seat is winnable, and they can promise campaign assistance if the potential candidate decides to take on the challenge. NRCC and DCCC leaders are evaluated according to their ability to convince strong candidates to run under their party label; candidate recruitment has become the most important job for party leaders.

Once the candidates are recruited, the job of the party organization shifts to providing campaign resources. Some of these resources are in the form of direct contributions, but the party is limited in how much it can assist candidates for federal office, to $5,000 for House candidates and $35,000 for Senate candidates. Equally important is the assistance they give to candidates in services. The parties do research and polling for candidates; they help them to hone their messages to voters, often producing generic ads that are used in districts around the country. The party committees also send surrogates into congressional districts to attract attention to candidates and to help them in their own fund-raising.

Perhaps the most important contribution that the party committees make is to tap a district as one that is in play. A party's decision to concentrate resources on a particular race is a signal to interest groups that share the party's views that they too should concentrate their efforts on that race. Party committees and leaders might be restricted in how much they can contribute to any one race, but they are not restricted in the ways in which they can assist candidates in networking—and that may well be their most valuable contribution. But even this is a resource that must not be squandered. The leaders of the Hill committees want to be certain that their allies allot their financial contributions strategically, so that money is concentrated on close races and not spent

unnecessarily either on those that are lost or those that will be easily won.

To a large extent, national party organization has become a core of an ongoing campaign staff poised to recruit and assist party candidates. The DNC and RNC exist as ongoing entities; they are the elected structure that is paraded out for show every few months. They do have the formal authority for the two parties; but only the two chairs have any national visibility and the staffs do the real politicking. Congressmen and Senators do hold seats on the DCCC and the NRCC, but only the chairs and the staffs perform identifiable roles. Those roles have virtually nothing to do with policy or governing and everything to do with fund-raising and politics. The national party organization exists in large part to serve the needs of its candidates.

State party organizations

Bill Roe was chair of the Arizona Democratic Party. Businessman Robert Graham was his Republican counterpart. Few people in Arizona knew that. In fact many state party websites do not even list the state chair. Who cares? Even the most active citizens have little contact with state committees; even the most active state chairs in the largest states have low political profiles.

This was not always the case. Some state party organizations had bosses as strong or stronger than those of local organizations, but with significant differences. Many state party bosses were U.S. senators. These state party machines were built in the days when U.S. senators were elected by state legislatures. Senators built organizations to secure their elections. One of the mechanisms they used to maintain their organizations was appointing followers to federal positions, and they were able to do this because of a long-standing tradition of senatorial courtesy. Senatorial courtesy meant that any U.S. senator could veto any federal

appointment in his state requiring confirmation by the Senate. Senators selected federal officeholders who worked to assure election of state legislators who would reelect the senator, quite a cozy arrangement.

The power of most of these senators and their organizations waned after the passage of the Seventeenth Amendment, but residual state machines persisted in one-party southern states for many decades. Typically, these organizations were led by demagogues whose initial appeal to the people gave way to autocratic rule. Some of the most colorful stories in American political history deal with the organization of Huey Long and his successors in Louisiana, Theodore Bilbo in Mississippi, and Gene Talmadge in Georgia.

Rejuvenation of state party organizations

Little of that color and little of the power remain in state party organizations of the twenty-first century. State party organizations parallel the national organization. Each has a state committee; the committee is comprised of representatives from local constituencies. The committees meet infrequently. The real work is done by the staff. Like the national parties, state parties have undergone a renaissance in the last half century. Fifty years ago many state party organizations were empty shells. Many states did not have permanent staff; few had permanent headquarters; budgets were meager and activities limited to the election season.

Today virtually every Democratic and Republican state party organization has a full-time paid staff; many have full-time paid chairs as well. State headquarters, which once moved around the state to the home city of the chair, are now typically permanent offices in the state capital. Budgets for the state organizations vary with the size of the state, as one would expect. But in every case the budget is enough to sustain ongoing political organizing, to prepare for election years, and to coordinate statewide campaigns.

Coordination of campaigns has been a key factor in the rejuvenation of state organizations. Federal election campaign finance laws restrict the amount of money that can be given to candidates for federal office. But these same laws permit expenditures for campaign activities that favor all of a party's candidates for offices. Thus, statewide political parties can maintain websites and coordinate statewide fund-raising and volunteer efforts; they can collect, process, and analyze voter information for all of their candidates; they can conduct polling for the party; they can run voter registration drives; they can do generic advertising; and they can run get-out-the-vote efforts. In an era of candidate-centered campaigning, fostered by candidates' necessary reliance on their own organizations to gain nomination through primaries, many high-budget campaigns carry out all of these activities; low-budget campaigns have to do without. But if the party can coordinate activities for their candidates, economies of scale are realized and donors who would be prohibited from giving additional money to a candidate can assist that candidate in other ways.

One mechanism through which this coordination works is the pass-through of money from one level of party organization to another. Table 3.2 (p. 64) shows the amount of money passed through by the Democratic and Republican National Committees to various state parties in 2012 in selected states. It is not surprising that the national parties invested more funds in states with competitive elections, allowing for more sophisticated campaigns in those areas.

Variations in state laws

In 2006 veteran U.S. senator Joseph Lieberman was challenged for his party's nomination for reelection by a Greenwich businessman, Ned Lamont. Party officials openly backed Lieberman in the primary. In a number of other states, either by party rule or custom, party leaders must stay neutral in all primaries. In still other states, the party officials may play a role in primaries, but the staff of the organization must stay neutral.

State party organizations differ from each other in a number of ways; most reflect the size and the partisan leanings of the state. But they also differ in terms of rules in a way that reflects on their roles. The roles in the primary process noted above fall into that category, with the party organization role going from neutrality, to informal endorsement, to formal endorsement at times by special placement or with a special designation on the ballot, to playing a formal role in the nominating process. In Connecticut as an example, the winner of the party endorsement is the nominee unless the party candidate is challenged in a primary by one of those who failed to get the party nod, as was the case with Lamont challenging Lieberman.

Party organization thus is one of the areas of American politics in which the nature of the federal system remains important. States differ from each other in important ways. Because of their differing histories and political cultures, their party systems differ significantly. And as a result of that, the role of party organization at the state level varies significantly. While it is true that the state party leaders are not well known to the public, the organizations that they head play important roles in campaign activities—more or less vital depending on the level of competition in the state. In all states party leaders recruit candidates for office, but in some states the role of the organization is far more important, actually selecting who will represent the party on the general election ballot.

Local party organizations

The strong local party organizations discussed at the beginning of this chapter provide material for legends, but the characters on which those legends are based have long since disappeared. Yet, local party organizations continue to exist and to play an important role in electoral politics.

American political parties have always been decentralized organizations; they begin at the grassroots and build to the

national level. Party committees are chosen at the precinct or town level; these committee members choose committee members for the next larger unit of governing, the ward in urban areas, often the county in rural areas. Party officials at these levels choose committee members for the state committees; state party leaders choose national committee members. The formal structure now differs little from that established more than 150 years ago.

The key question has always revolved around the locus of power. In the days of the powerful boss, the power rested with the public official who controlled jobs—often the mayor or county executive, always someone whose tenure in office depended on the party boss. In some states, U.S. senators held the power, but more often a series of local leaders were clearly the most powerful. National party leaders were always seen as weak, with few resources and little influence. Their job was often to broker agreements among the powerful, and autonomous, local and state leaders.

Today power, to the extent that party power exists, stems from control over money. Most of the money to run party organizations is raised at the national level. State leaders and to an even greater extent local leaders are dependent on the expertise and often largesse of national leaders.

But that is not to say that the roles played by local leaders are unimportant. The roles that they play are the traditional roles of political parties. They recruit candidates and fill slots on the ticket. They coordinate volunteers and energize the party faithful. They advertise for their candidates and do the one-on-one campaigning that is often still critical in local elections. They work hard to get their loyal supporters, the party base, out to vote. A generation ago this work was incredibly labor intensive. Local parties needed armies of volunteers to maintain voter lists, to address envelopes, to make telephone calls, to drop literature.

If any electioneering today is done personally, it is still done at the local level. But it has certainly been eased by the age of Internet communication. Even at the most local level, party organizations maintain websites; volunteers receive frequent electronic updates on campaign progress; volunteers are coordinated and their activities tracked electronically. Campaigns still leaflet neighborhoods and accompany candidates on door-to-door visits to voters, but the armies of volunteers are coordinated through careful tracking of a database of those committed to a party or a candidate. The national campaigns in recent cycles have demonstrated the effectiveness of electronic means for fund-raising and volunteer communication and coordination. These lessons have not been lost on local party organizations, even the least sophisticated of which have copied many of Dean's techniques.

Party conventions

One could argue that the high point of Mitt Romney's 2012 campaign for the presidency came when he strode to the stage of the Republican National Convention in Tampa, Florida, and basked in the adulation of those who weathered the threat of Hurricane Isaac to crown him their nominee. The Romney campaign orchestrated the convention's message, coalescing the party and showcasing their candidate and his family to the nation. But, it should also be remembered that no major party decisions were made at that convention. The nominee was known in advance, chosen as delegates pledged to Romney were selected earlier in the year. Romney chose his running mate, Wisconsin congressman Paul Ryan. The Romney campaign monitored the platform-writing process to assure that the party's official views and the candidate's were in line.

In both major political parties, the national conventions stand at the pinnacle of the party's formal decision making, but in practice few decisions are made there. Conventions do retain very real functions however. In part, those are solidary functions. The

conventions are a time when the party faithful can come together, enjoy an atmosphere of unity, rejoice in the party's past, and plan together for the glorious future, which is about to unfold. But more substantively, the conventions of the two national parties set the rules under which the parties function, including the rules that will govern subsequent nominating processes.

In addition, the party conventions do pass platforms that lay out the party's positions on the issues of the day. At times the debates before the party platform committee reflect broader philosophical debates within the party. At other times, the platform writing is tightly controlled by the nominee's followers. While American political leaders are not committed to follow the mandates of the party platform as are leaders of parliamentary democracies, party platforms go a good way toward defining the parties in the eyes of the electorate. Thus, presumptive presidential candidates have worked hard to dominate the platform-writing process. They do not want to be saddled with a platform that takes controversial positions to which they are not wed.

The 1992 national party platforms

By the time the two national parties named their Platform Committees in 1992, it was clear that President George H. W. Bush would be re-nominated by the Republicans and that Bill Clinton would be the Democratic nominee.

The Republicans allowed the social conservative wing of the party to dominate the platform-writing process. Bush's campaign aides determined that the platform's content was not as important as keeping the conservatives solidly behind their candidate. As a result, the 1992 GOP platform took extreme positions on many of the controversial social issues of the day.

By contrast, Bill Clinton's advisors wanted to be certain that the Democrats' platform represented his centrist views, the views

promulgated by the Democratic Leadership Council. They lobbied hard to name the chairs of the Platform Committee and the leader of the drafting subcommittee, and for Clinton supporters to dominate the committee membership. The Clinton leadership team (Rep. Nancy Pelosi of California and Gov. Roy Roemer of Colorado for the full committee; Rep. Bill Richardson of New Mexico for the Drafting Committee) negotiated with the Democratic contenders who had lost to Clinton to assure that the platform would represent the nominee's views and that the losing candidates would not challenge any planks on the floor.

The result was telling. The Republican convention divided over platform issues; the party looked to be in the hands of social extremists, and moderates were disheartened. The Democrats united behind their nominee with a unifying moderate platform. These images carried over into the general election.

State party conventions vary according to the role that the party plays in the nominating process. If the party role is pivotal, then campaigns vie to have delegates pledged to them seated and voting. These conventions are often contentious. Candidate differences are reflected in rules fights, in platform fights, in shows of support. When the convention eventually endorses a nominee, the party either demonstrates unity or remains divided, depending on whether the convention's endorsement is likely to be challenged in a primary.

In other states, party conventions are simply displays of party unity. Party regulars come together to be energized by officeholders seeking to stir the faithful to participate in their campaigns. Platforms are adopted but are often meaningless. The main purpose of these conventions is as a kickoff to the fall campaign, a pep rally to prepare the troops for the effort ahead.

Summary

Political party organizations in the United States reflect the nation's federal system. The party is organized at each electoral level. What is constant is that the real work of the party is done by staff, and the principle role of the party is to assist their candidates for office. Formal party organization does not define party positions. The leaders of the party organization are not able to discipline public officials elected under the party label. Rather, the strength of the party is directly related to its ability to assist in campaign functions. The current situation is a far cry from the role played by party organization a century ago, reflecting important changes in the critical aspects of the electoral process—the stakes of the game, the incentives for participation, and the means used to reach voters.

Chapter 4

Who are Republicans?
Who are Democrats?
Who are the "others"?

If you look at prominent figures, these questions are easy to answer. President Barack Obama is a Democrat; Speaker of the House Paul Ryan, a Republican. Public officials run as nominees of one party or the other. But what about the school teacher in Vermont, the textile worker in North Carolina, the farmer in Nebraska, the computer engineer in California? Are they Democrats or Republicans? Who are the independents, and who represents them in government?

For generations, political scientists have found it useful to distinguish among the party in the electorate, the party organization, and the party in government. The party in the electorate is the voters; the party organization is comprised of those individuals who run for and serve on, or who are employed by, party committees at the local, state, and national levels. The party in government is comprised of public officials, elected or appointed, who are identified with one major party or the other as they serve.

We explore party affiliation in each of those three contexts. We will show how party in the electorate is a moving target. However defined, voters who identify with the major parties are easily distinguishable from those who work for the parties or run or are appointed as representatives of the parties.

Party in the electorate

How do you know if someone is a Democrat or a Republican? What does it mean to be a Democrat or a Republican? We know that party membership in the United States does not mean what it does in Europe. That is, Americans do not join a political party in any real sense; parties do not maintain membership rolls. We also know that party allegiance is the single best predictor of a citizen's vote. Democrats, *ceteris paribus*—other things being equal—vote for Democrats; Republicans, for Republicans.

The party in the electorate is normally analyzed in one of three ways. The first is to examine those who are enrolled in one major party or the other. This means is limited, however, because many states do not maintain official lists of party enrollees. If one says one is a Democrat in Maine, for example, it signifies that a citizen is enrolled in the Democratic party and that that voter is eligible to vote in the Democratic primary. However, if that voter's sister says she is a Republican in Wisconsin, the meaning is different. The state of Wisconsin does not enroll voters in one party or another; she can vote in either party's primary. Because of state-by-state variation in the election law, party enrollment is not a very useful analytical concept.

The second method is to analyze those people who vote for the Republican or the Democratic candidate. This definition of party identification is in some ways the most meaningful; after all, we are concerned with election outcomes. Thus it makes sense to analyze how those who supported President Obama differed from those who supported Governor Romney. If our goal is to understand the result of a specific election, then examining the supporters of the candidates in that election makes a good deal of sense. But those who vote for the Democratic candidate for one office often vote for the Republican candidate for another office. On a long ballot, voters might well switch back and forth between

the parties. Furthermore, those who support the Republican candidate for a particular office in one year often support the Democratic candidate in the next election. If our concern is to understand which voters are Republicans and which are Democrats, voting behavior is a limited tool. We hear often that more and more citizens are independents. On election day these voters are often faced with only two choices—a Democrat or a Republican. How can we understand their behavior if we eliminate them by definition?

As a result of these limitations, political scientists most often use a third mode of analysis, the concept of party identification, to examine which voters are Democrats and which, Republicans. Party identification is a concept that measures a voter's self assessment of their allegiance to one party or another. As such it is different from either party membership or voting for candidates of a party.

Various polling organizations have measured party identification over the years. Commercial pollsters, such as Gallup, generally report how the electorate divides itself among Democrats, independents, and Republicans. The question asked is quite simple: "In politics, as of today, do you consider yourself a Republican, a Democrat, or an independent?" (Asked of independents: "As of today, do you lean more to the Democratic Party or the Republican Party?")

For many years the Democrats had a significant advantage, with few voters declaring their independence from the major parties. In the last decade, the Republicans have closed the gap between them and the Democrats, and many more voters list themselves as independent. As a result, nearly equal numbers of voters place themselves in each category, with small numbers switching from month to month. In a Gallup Poll conducted in June 2015, 31 percent identified themselves as Democrats, 25 percent as Republicans, and 41 percent as independents. When

"leaners" were taken into account, that is assigning those who say they lean toward one party or the other to that party, Democratic identifiers outnumbered Republicans but by only 45 percent to 43 percent.

Political scientists tend to rely more heavily on the National Election Studies (NES) that have asked similar questions of voters in surveys conducted surrounding every presidential election since that of 1952. The NES question regarding party affiliation is "Generally speaking, do you usually think of yourself as a Republican, a Democrat, an independent, or what?" Because the NES surveys probed far more deeply into respondent characteristics than do commercial surveys, they are far more useful in coming to an understanding of the electorate.

Party identification is useful in answering the question about who are the Republicans, who are the Democrats, and who are the "others" in at least two ways. The first is to look at various groups in society in order to determine whether members of particular groups tend to see themselves in one party or the other. The other means is to look at the party coalitions, to determine to what degree specific groups contribute to each party's followers.

Analyzing the affiliations of political groups

Political parties often appeal to voters based on their group membership. The New Deal coalition, the combination of groups that supported the Democratic party after the 1932 election of Franklin Delano Roosevelt, was comprised of white southerners, urban working-class Americans, especially union members, African Americans, Jews, and Catholics. The Republicans' coalition was more difficult to define, but surely non-poor whites and citizens of small towns and rural areas made important contributions. That picture held for more than thirty years, but changes were clearly seen in the last decades of the twentieth century that have persisted into the twenty-first.

Some groups' support for the Democrats clearly declined. The extreme example of such a group is native white southerners. Native white southerners identified with the Democratic Party in very large numbers until the 1960s. While they might have opposed liberal Democratic policies, particularly on the question of civil rights, the Republican party did not compete for major offices in the South until after the 1964 election, so white southerners had nowhere to go but to the Democrats. By the 1980s the allegiance of this group had changed dramatically; today native white southerners are much more likely to identify with the Republicans than with the Democrats.

Catholics were an important part of the New Deal coalition. Their allegiance to the Democrats was strengthened by the candidacy and election of John F. Kennedy, the first Roman Catholic elected to the White House. Today Catholics are only slightly more likely to identify themselves as Democrats than as Republicans; the Catholic vote was very closely dividided the first four presidential elections of this century. Union members are just as likely to be Democrats as they have traditionally been, but many fewer workers are members of unions. The allegiance of blacks and Jews to the Democratic Party has remained virtually constant over the last half century.

Some groups have emerged to be important in American politics in the late twentieth and early twenty-first centuries that were not deemed significant a generation or two ago. Hispanics stand out because they will soon comprise the largest minority group in the nation. Currently the Democrats have a significant advantage in gaining the Hispanic vote. Hispanics favor the Democrats over the Republicans by almost three to one, though the percentage has varied from election to election. In part this variation is a reflection of competing group allegiance. Many Hispanics are also religious fundamentalists and regular churchgoers—two other groups not isolated for their political relevance in the past. Each of these groups heavily favors the Republican party. Hispanics who

fall into these categories, those who might favor the Democrats for other reasons, are torn. However, the Republican party stance on immigration policy, opposed by most Hispanics, has hindered their efforts to make inroads into this group most recently.

The important questions about group allegiance deal first with why members of a particular group were attracted to a party as members of that group in the first place, and then with why they continue to identify with that party, lose their allegiance but stay neutral, or switch to the other party.

Group allegiance forms because of policies put forth by political leaders of a specific political party. The *New York Times* columnist David Brooks made this point cogently in a column titled "Losing Alito," published at the time of the Supreme Court justice's confirmation hearing. Had Samuel Alito been born a decade earlier, Brooks asserts, he, like other urban ethnic Americans, would have been a Democrat. But the Democrats lost the Alitos of this world.

> Democrats did their best to repel Northern white ethnic voters. Big-city liberals launched crusades against police brutality, portraying working-class cops as thuggish storm troopers for the establishment. In the media, educated liberals portrayed urban ethnics as uncultured, uneducated Archie Bunkers. The liberals were doves; the ethnics were hawks. The liberals had "Question Authority" bumper stickers; the ethnics had been taught in school to respect authority. The liberals thought an unjust society caused poverty; the ethnics believed in working their way out of poverty.

A parallel argument could be made concerning some groups that support Republicans. Establishment nonfundamentalist Protestants find the domination of their party by the religious right to be troubling; they think they have less and less in common with those running their party.

The logical next question is why the parties act in these ways, a question we will return to in the discussion of party organization and party in government.

Party coalitions

Group contribution to a party coalition is a function of the percentage of those in a certain group who affiliate with a political party and of the overall size of the group. Thus, Jews are overwhelmingly Democrats but make up a very small percentage of the voting public and thus a small percentage of the Democratic coalition, approximately 5 percent. Nearly two-thirds of all Democrats are women; here we see the much-discussed gender gap as less than half of the Republicans are female. Catholics make up about a quarter of the Democratic coalition and about the same percentage of the GOP coalition. By contrast blacks account for about 22 percent of all Democrats, but only 2 percent of Republicans.

What distinguishes the Republican coalition from the Democrats? Clearly, race is one factor. Democratic party identifiers are much more likely to be of a minority race (about 40 percent) than are Republican identifiers (about 8 percent). Gender is another factor, with a gap of more than 10 percent among female party identifiers. The party coalitions are also distinguished by income. Nearly 40 percent of those who report themselves to be Republican are in the top one-third of the income distribution in the nation; fewer than 30 percent of the Democrats achieve that level. Southern whites now comprise one-third of all Republicans, but only about one-sixth of the Democrats. Finally, religious beliefs distinguish the two groups. A higher percentage of Republicans attend church regularly than is true of Democrats (42 percent – 34 percent); more strikingly, nearly one in six Republicans assert that they are fundamentalist Christians; only 7 percent of the Democrats claim those beliefs. The contrast between these views of the two parties and the New Deal Coalition could hardly be more stark.

The party organization

The Republicans and Democrats who populate their respective party organizations are self-selected activists. They are all but unknown to the general public. They attend committee meetings and plan campaigns. They draft platforms and do the nitty-gritty work of campaigning. Generally they are more concerned with local politics than with state or national politics. Partisan victory is important to them.

They are also the true believers in the party. Systematic studies of these party activists have reached similar conclusions. Whereas once party organization was synonymous with material incentives, in the contemporary context, those who run for positions in the party organization or who work for the party are more concerned with policy than patronage.

What policy? For the Democrats, party activists and staff tend to be more liberal than the average Democrat, more committed to traditional liberal Democratic policies. For the Republicans, core activists tend to be more conservative. In recent years, this conservatism has been social conservatism more than economic conservatism. Evangelical Christians have made a concerted and a successful effort to capture party machinery in a number of states and have made inroads in others.

If one assumes that it is possible to view public opinion on political issues along a spectrum from conservative on the right to liberal on the left, and if one further assumes that a normal curve defines the spread of public opinion on that spectrum, party activists tend to find themselves at the extremes, and rank-and-file party identifiers tend to occupy positions closer to the center. The more active one is in the party, the more likely one is to hold extreme positions, particularly on the most salient issues of the day. Thus, Democratic party officers are likely to be more liberal than those

who merely vote in primaries; primary voters are likely to be more liberal than Democratic identifiers who do not bother to turn out for primary elections.

One could certainly claim an inconsistency here. If a primary goal is partisan victory, then party activists should want their party to assume centrist positions, for these would appeal to more voters and lead to victory. However, if one is a committed believer to more extreme policy positions, another logic holds: it is necessary to convince others that your position is correct, to control the party machinery, to nominate candidates who share your view, and to mobilize others with similar opinions to support those candidates in order to have those views prevail.

Certain consequences for the electoral system follow. First, the more influential party organization is in the process, the less likely it is that compromise positions will be taken. Second, the more one party dominates a geographic area, the more valuable the nomination is and the more potential candidates will appeal to the party base, not to the center. As a result, officeholders from one-party areas tend to be more partisan and extreme on controversial issues than are those from more competitive areas. Third, official party positions, for example, those taken in party platforms that are written largely by party activists, tend to emphasize salient issues on which the parties differ, not those on which compromise positions are possible. Taken together then, one sees that the activists in party organizations contribute to increasingly divided and bitter partisanship.

Party organization in the golden era of parties, a century ago, was concerned with gaining power and the spoils that went with that power. Party leaders were often towering political figures. Those who worked under them were bound to them and to the organization because of the patronage they controlled. Local politics was more important than state or national politics, because more patronage was controlled at the local level. Party positions were decidedly secondary.

In the twenty-first century, party leaders are largely unknown except for by other activists in their local area, they still perform the traditional party functions, but their motivation for supporting the party is because of policy preferences, not because of potential patronage. Party positions are not valued for personal gain. As a result, those who care most about policy are able to capture party posts and dominate the organizations.

The party in government

President Obama and Speaker Ryan stand as obvious examples of politicians associated with their political party. When one refers to well-known politicians, those who follow politics even remotely can conjure up certain images. President Obama stands for ending the wars in Iraq and Afghanistan and for affordable healthcare. Speaker Ryan is associated with fiscal conservatism, strengthening national defense, stricter immigration laws, and a smaller government. The images may not be precise, but they are clear nonetheless.

How clear are the distinctions between Democrats and Republicans in office? To a large extent that depends on what level of precision you seek. A generation ago, even the most astute observers would have difficulty defining what it meant to be a Democratic officeholder. Democratic Senator Ted Kennedy took an extremely liberal position on most issues. But Governor George C. Wallace of Alabama, who ran for president as a Democrat, symbolized southern conservative Democrats, of whom there were many. Washington State was represented in the Senate by Henry M. Jackson, a liberal on domestic policies but a staunch conservative on defense matters. During the Vietnam War, Democrat Lyndon Johnson led the war effort, with many allies in the Congress, including most Republicans; other Democrats led opposition to the war, along with a few Republicans. It was difficult to define where the party in government stood.

In the first decade of the twenty-first century, defining the party in government seems to be somewhat easier, at least at the national level. For each session of Congress, the Congressional Quarterly Service computes a Party Unity Score for each Representative and Senator. In the most recent congresses, each party's average unity score has been over 90 percent; the percentage of votes on which a majority of one party opposed a majority of the other has also increased. In Congress generally one finds the Democrats supporting President Obama, and Republicans opposing a large portion of his initiatives.

Some variation does exist if one looks at the state or regional level. In the Republican party, as a clear example, party officeholders from New England tend to be moderate on social issues; those from states in the Bible Belt, the religiously conservative area in the heartland of the country, tend to be much more conservative. For much of the twentieth century the Republicans were a more homogeneous party than the Democrats; in recent years, however, Republicans have become more split, with the division occurring around social issues on the agenda.

This change can be seen around the issue of abortion. In 1992 Pennsylvania's Democratic governor Robert P. Casey was not permitted to air his pro-life views at the Democratic National Convention. In 2006, his pro-life son, Robert P. Casey, Jr., was sought out by party leaders to be their candidate for the U.S. Senate. At the same time, the Republican party is defined more as a pro-life party, with little divergence tolerated. Former Massachusetts governor Mitt Romney, who equivocated on his stand on abortion rights when running for office in a liberal state, made determined efforts to stake out firmly pro-life positions when he decided to explore the Republican presidential nomination.

Even with these variations noted, however, Democrats in government and Republicans in government are easily

identifiable—and in fact go to great efforts to separate themselves. On issue after issue, when one party's leaders take a stand, those of the other party take the opposite stand. At the national level at least, the issues on which officeholders from the two parties work together to find common solutions are few and far between. Partisan conflict is much more prevalent than partisan cooperation; divisiveness is much more common than a search for mutually acceptable solutions to pressing problems.

The independents

In looking at who are Democrats and who are Republicans, we have not dealt with the residual group—who are the independents. For the party in government, that is easiest to answer: there are very few of them. When the 114th Congress convened in 2015, Bernie Sanders of Vermont and Angus King of Maine were the only independent senators, and no independents served in the House of Representatives. Bill Walker of Alaska was the only governor who was neither a Democrat nor a Republican. Approximately 99 percent of the state legislators were also affiliated with one or the other of the two major parties.

Party organization for independents is oxymoronic. How can there be a party organization if there is no party? However, when independent candidates run, they do form organizations. Most of those are episodic, coming together for one campaign and then disbanding. They are the followers of the candidate, often following him or her for the same reason the candidate is running—concern for one issue or a set of issues, dissatisfaction with the established candidates. Occasionally such an organization persists, as did H. Ross Perot's organization after his 1992 bid for the presidency. These followers might try to form a new party or to continue following the leader who drew them to politics. They—like those who labor for minor parties that have persisted over time—are dedicated to a cause but rarely influential in the process.

Independents in the electorate often determine the outcome of an election. They are not a unified group. Some are very involved in politics but choose not to affiliate with one party or the other, because their views are not in line with either party's views. Others, once affiliated with one party, have become disenchanted but are not willing to move to the other side. Still others are interested in politics but disapprove of politicians who are too partisan to maintain their independence. Finally, a large group are uninterested in politics or government policy and do not identify with either party because they are not concerned enough to follow the discussions. Thus, some of the independents are among the most informed and most concerned of citizens; others are among the least informed and least concerned. Candidates must be aware of both groups and determine how to make appropriate, effective appeals. Making this judgment is often more art than science and based more on emotion than substance. Often, in the relatively few competitive races that do exist, those judgments separate winners from losers.

Summary

Political parties are central to American elections, but party membership in any formal sense is alien to most citizens. Indeed, many have no formal affiliation; many do not even identify with one party or the other. Nonetheless, the concept of party remains important. Most citizens have an impression of the two major parties, of what they stand for, of what kinds of citizens think of themselves as part of each party. Even those who consider themselves to be independents most often vote for candidates who are either Democrats or Republicans—and they often do so because they have a sense of what it means to be a candidate of one party or the other. Candidates run with the support of party organizations. While they may seek independence from those organizations, none denies rather than none deny, particularly in recruiting candidates and in raising money in close races. In close races, party organizations also play crucial roles in

assuring that supporters turn out to vote. Finally, once politicians are elected, they organize themselves in governing by political party. Elected officials are identified by their party label and are thought to act in certain ways, because they are Democrats or Republicans. An increasingly large number of citizens claim allegiance to neither party and take pride in their independence. What this frequently means is that they switch from supporting candidates of one party to those of another, not that they have discovered a third path into American politics.

Chapter 5
Presidential elections: Nominating campaigns and general elections

In November and December 2000, when citizens of the world waited for weeks to find out whether George W. Bush or Al Gore had won the American presidential election, analysts and citizens agreed on two observations. First, the system was terribly flawed. A country that views itself as a beacon of democracy, a model for nations emerging as democracies, could not be proud of an electoral system that left the result in doubt for weeks, with the clear implication that the winner would be determined based on judicial interpretations of questionable ballots.

Second, few people truly understood the system. Not only Americans but also those throughout the world who point to the democratic principles of the United States as ideals to be emulated were amazed to learn that George W. Bush might be elected even though Albert Gore received more votes. Throughout the United States civics teachers were talking to their students about the Electoral College, and those students were going home explaining it to their parents. Television journalists who did understand the system stumbled often as they tried to explain it to their audiences.

If the means by which citizens of the United States elect their president is complex, flawed, and misunderstood, the means through which the two major parties choose their nominees is even

more so. Citizens know that the nominees are chosen at party conventions, but they also know that the identity of the nominee is known well in advance of those gatherings. How? Which states have primaries and which caucuses—and what difference does it make? How do they work? Who are the delegates to the conventions? How are they chosen? What do they do?

The nominating process is not some abstraction, of interest only to political junkies. The way in which the nominating process works determines which candidates will be viable and which have no chance. This process winnows the field of potential presidents from a large number down to two—the two major party nominees. One cannot understand the results of American elections if one does not understand how the candidates are chosen.

Similarly, the rules of the general election are not neutral. The Electoral College system favors some candidates and disadvantages others. George Bush was elected because of how this system works. He might not have been elected had an alternative system been in place. Candidate strategies would have changed had the rules been different. Financial backing plays a huge role in presidential nominations and elections; campaign contributions are regulated—and the strength or weakness of these regulations also contributes to determining who will win and who will lose. One can only critique the system in terms of democratic values if one understands the ways in which it functions and the likely consequences of alternatives.

The nominating process

Barack Obama was twice nominated by the Democratic Party as their candidate for the presidency, in 2008, when President George W. Bush was leaving the White House, and in 2012, when seeking reelection. Those two nominations stand as examples of two of the possible varieties in a typology of party nominations for president. Mitt Romney's nomination in 2012, the

Republican nomination to oppose an incumbent Democrat, stands as a third type.

Table 5.1 presents a number of variables that one must consider in analyzing presidential nominations. The key contextual variable is the presence or absence of an incumbent president seeking reelection. Related to that is the second factor, whether the nomination under examination is for the nod of the party of the incumbent or for the "out" party nomination. The process clearly runs differently if one candidate is the presumptive nominee early in the nominating season from those instances in which no such favorite emerges.

A number of conclusions about intraparty competition can be drawn from this figure. First, few nominations other than those for reelection have gone to candidates who were presumptive nominees early in the campaign season. And those four are of interest. Two were to run against incumbent presidents thought to be invulnerable; that is, the nominations were not seen as very valuable. Walter Mondale in 1984 and Bob Dole in 1996 were each respected party leaders who, in a sense, were due the nomination; however, it is likely that they would have been more strongly challenged within their own parties if other potential candidates thought that the sitting president seeking reelection might lose. Al Gore in 2000 was a sitting vice president and heir apparent; he was to carry on the legacy of the Clinton-Gore team.

But the nomination of George W. Bush in 2000 is quite different. Bush was all but anointed by party leaders—not the formal party organization but elected leaders within the party, including Republican governors, and major contributors to the party, including many in his native Texas. He became the presumptive nominee because he had such a huge advantage going into the actual primary season, a financial advantage that caused many other potentially serious contenders to drop out.

Table 5.1 Typology of competition for presidential nominations (with number of serious contenders for the nomination in parentheses)

	Party of nominee			
	Incumbent's Party		Other party	
Presidential context	Presumptive nominee	No presumptive nominee	Presumptive nominee	No presumptive nominee
Seeking Reelection	Nixon, 1972 Reagan, 1984 Clinton, 1996 Bush, 2004 Obama, 2012	Ford, 1976 (2) Carter, 1980 (2) Bush, 1992 (2)	Mondale, 1984 (6) Dole, 1996 (5)	McGovern, 1972 (8) Carter, 1976 (10) Reagan, 1980 (7) Clinton, 1992 (7) Kerry, 2004 (6)
				Romney, 2012 (8)
Not Seeking Reelection	Gore, 2000 (2)	Bush, 1988 (6) McCain, 2008 (8)	Bush, 2000 (6)	Dukakis, 1988 (7) Obama, 2008 (3)

The 2008 Democratic nomination is perhaps the starkest case in recent years in which the front runner at the beginning of primary season did not ultimately go on to win the nomination. With an initial advantage, both monetarily and in the polls, Hillary Clinton was the clear front runner in the lead-up to election year. However, as Barack Obama gradually caught up to—and eventually surpassed—Clinton in fund-raising and went on to win the Iowa caucuses, the inevitability of Clinton's nomination fell into doubt. Still, the contest would remain competitive throughout primary season, until Clinton conceded the race in June.

It is important to look at the strategies of candidates who run in different contexts. Before one can understand the strategies, however, it is necessary to have a sense of the rules under which these campaigns are run.

The rules of the game

The bottom line is simple: The presidential nominee of a party is that candidate who receives a majority of the votes cast on one ballot at his or her party's nominating convention. The vice presidential nominee is that candidate who receives a majority of the votes for vice president at the nominating convention. What could be simpler?

For more than half a century, the nominating conventions have been the frosting on the cake. Delegates chosen well in advance of the convention are pledged to one candidate or another. The nominee becomes clear once one candidate has accumulated enough pledged delegates to guarantee that majority vote. And, to complete the ticket, the delegates routinely vote for the candidate for vice president suggested to them by the presidential candidate.

Who then are these delegates and how are they chosen? The two major parties differ in a number of important details as to how they apportion delegates among the states and as to how

the actual delegates are chosen. Each party has a formula that determines how many delegates each state should send to its national convention; the formulas, which can change from convention to convention, are generally based on two factors—voting population of the state, and the party's success in recent elections within the state. The Democrats also assure that certain groups of elected officials are represented as delegates on the convention floor—members of Congress, governors, state officials, party leaders, and the like. Democratic National Conventions are generally larger than Republican National Conventions.

Means of selecting delegates also vary between the parties and, within the parties, among the states. Generally, the Republicans give state party organizations more leeway in selecting the means through which delegates are chosen; the Democrats impose certain guidelines on state leaders.

Two principle means are used to select delegates, presidential preference primaries and caucuses. In a presidential preference *primary*, the names of the candidates for a party's nomination appear on the ballot, and citizens cast a vote for one of the candidates. The results of this vote are used to select the actual delegates who attend the convention. Again, it seems simple, but the variations in systems reveal how complex it is.

First, who are the citizens who vote? Is every registered voter eligible or just those who are members of the party? What is meant by "member of the party," in an organization that has no formal membership? Some states, Wisconsin as an example, have so-called open primaries, primaries in which any registered voter may participate. Other states like New Hampshire permit independents who have not enrolled in either party to vote in either party's primary, but Democrats cannot vote in the Republican primary, and Republicans cannot vote in the Democrats'. Still other states, like Maryland or New York, have closed primaries, primaries in which

only those who have enrolled in one of the major parties or the other may vote, effectively excluding independents from participation. States vary in enough ways that a continuum exists between open and closed systems, with few states running pure primaries of either type.

Those who believe in democracy, the rule of the people, in its purest form should favor more open systems, right? Not so fast. In an open system Democrats might determine who the Republicans' nominee should be. Isn't that a decision that Republicans should make? If party means anything, does it not seem right that those who adhere to the party's principles should choose its candidates? That logic argues for a more closed system.

The same logic also argues that a more open system, with citizens crossing party lines to vote in a primary election, should lead to more centrist candidates. Candidates in primary elections would have to appeal across party lines. A more closed system would lead to candidates whose views were more divergent, easier for the voters to distinguish in the general election, but some might also claim, more extreme. Choices in rules lead to differences in outcomes.

A second variation deals with who wins the primary. A prior question to that concerns the geographic size of the voting area. Delegates may be elected to the national convention from districts or they may be elected statewide—or, a state may opt for a combination of the two. Within whatever unit is chosen, in the Democratic party, delegates to the national convention are divided among the candidates proportionately according to the percentage of votes received in the primary. In the Republican party, the Democrats' system of proportional representation is used in some states, but in other states the winner of the primary wins all of the delegates.

Again, which system is to be preferred? Which is "fairer" or "better" is not clear. A system of proportional representation allows the

district or state delegation to the national convention to reflect the voting preferences of those who cast primary votes more precisely. That certainly is a valid goal for a voting system. But a winner-take-all system allows a front-running candidate to cement a lead more quickly, to unify the party behind his or her candidacy, and perhaps to have an advantage going into the general election. That too is a valid goal for a primary voting system. The trade-off between a system more likely to produce a winner in the general election and one that is more democratic is one that has separated party professionals from party reformers for decades. That battle has been fought openly in the Democratic party in a series of reform commissions that have struggled with party governance, rules, and procedures. The Republicans have been very willing to let Democrats battle internally over this while they use a system that has more often than not produced candidates leading a unified party.

In 2012, thirty-three of the fifty states chose national convention delegates by primary election in the Democratic party; thirty-six of the fifty did so in the Republican party. Of the 5,552 delegates to the Democratic convention, almost 80 percent were chosen in primaries; about 83 percent of the Republican delegates were chosen in primaries. The rest were chosen in caucuses.

Caucuses are essentially meetings of party members, people who are enrolled in one party or the other. In caucus states, party members throughout the state gather in their home locales on the same day. At these local caucuses, representatives of the various contending candidates make the best case they can, and then those assembled discuss the campaign and the strengths and weaknesses of the contenders and vote openly for their choice. The outcome of a local caucus is the election of delegates to a county or state convention, pledged to the various candidates in proportion to their support at the caucus. Caucus attendance is generally much lower than primary turnout. However,

8. Officials tally votes at the presidential primary in Dixville Notch, New Hampshire, traditionally the first town in the state to report its results.

caucus supporters argue that the level of commitment to
the process demonstrated by attending a meeting that might
last a number of hours and discussing the campaign
argues for the merits of this system of choosing among
candidates.

The most contentious issue debated by those who analyze the
presidential nominating process relates to the calendar of events.
For more than half a century, the New Hampshire primary has
been held before any others; for nearly as long, the Iowa
caucuses have opened the official nominating season. Leading
candidates tend to concentrate on these contests, giving those
states significant influence, many argue too much influence for
states that are unrepresentative of the nation as a whole or of
the supporters of either party. States, either acting on their own or
in consort with other states from their same region, have

moved their primary or caucus dates to early in the process in order to increase the attention paid to their contests. As a result, the entire nominating process is "front-loaded."

However, the 2008 Democratic nominating contests revealed a shift in primary season strategy. Rather than focusing exclusively on the states with the earliest contests, Barack Obama competed in every race and scored delegates in many smaller, caucus states, while Hillary Clinton focused almost solely on bigger states. Their differing strategies were clear in the results: In total, Clinton won twelve more delegates than Obama in primaries, but Obama collected 153 more than Clinton in caucuses, allowing him to upset Clinton, the front runner, in a long—and expensive—nominating season, lasting from the first caucuses in Iowa in January to the last primaries in South Dakota and Montana in June.

Strategic considerations

Increasingly, money motivates strategic decisions. In an effort to compete in almost every state's nominating contests in 2008, the Obama campaign revolutionized the use of the Internet, building a massive grassroots organization online and attracting millions of small donors to overcome Clinton's initial monetary advantage.

Primary campaigns are funded in one of two ways. The Federal Election Campaign Act (FECA) calls for matching public funds to pay for the presidential primaries. Nearly all candidates opted for this means of funding their nominations from the time that the act took effect in 1976 until the 2000 nomination of George W. Bush. The system was viewed as successful in keeping the escalating cost of nominating contests in check and in leveling the playing fields among the contenders.

Strategies changed in 2000, however. Then–Texas governor George W. Bush adopted a preemptive approach, using the other means of funding primary campaigns—by raising money privately, without restrictions on subsequent spending. Building a coalition

of party leaders that included elected officials (especially his fellow Republican governors), supporters from his father's campaigns, and wealthy Texans, Bush raised more money than had been thought possible before that time, $70 million before the first primary vote had been cast. A number of prominent Republicans who had considered running for the nomination, such as former Tennessee governor Lamar Alexander and former cabinet secretary Elizabeth Dole, dropped out before Iowa and New Hampshire, recognizing that they did not have the ability to compete for resources with the Texas governor. Observers worried that the effectiveness of the FECA was destroyed and that big money would once more dominate presidential politics.

In part they were right, but in part fundraisers for candidates for presidential nominations adjusted with ingenuity. They are also right in that money as a resource has become a key element in presidential nominating contests, in a very different way from what it was between 1976 and 2000. In the early period, candidates used qualification for federal matching funds as a means of demonstrating the viability of their candidacies. Today, candidates must make a decision whether they will use the matching-fund route or raise more money on their own, knowing full well that at least some candidates will raise private money and thus be permitted to spend more than those running federally funded campaigns. The decision is both practical and strategic. In a practical sense, can they raise significantly more than the federal matching sum would give them? In a strategic sense, do they want to be viewed as someone raising and spending huge sums of money? To succeed does their campaign need to spend money in ways prohibited to federally funded candidates, such as by exceeding the limit imposed in some states?

However, those who worried about the move to private funding necessarily thinking that campaigns would be dominated by those who could raise money from donors with huge bankrolls were wrong. Relying on private wealth, as Steve Forbes did in 1996 and

2000, or on contributions from wealthy individuals, as Bush did in 2000, were the known means to raise huge sums of money. Countering that, first John McCain, in the 2000 GOP primaries, and then Howard Dean and later John Kerry, in the run-up to the 2004 Democratic nomination, demonstrated that the Internet could be used to generate large sums of money in relatively small donations from hundreds of thousands of citizens. Candidates must now make decisions regarding whether their candidacy is the type that would appeal to an electorate likely to support them in this way.

Beyond the decisions regarding how to fund their campaigns, the most important strategic decisions by candidates for presidential nominations and their staffs involve where to campaign and how much of their effort should be devoted to which states. These decisions are governed by the resources available, the rules in effect in each state, the ideology of the candidate and the electorate in each state, and the calendar.

Candidates with more money can campaign effectively in more states; candidates with more limited resources—either financial or in terms of staff and organization (which is often a function of money)—must decide to concentrate their efforts on some states and to forgo others. Candidates with a wider appeal, especially an appeal to independents, concentrate their efforts in states with open primaries; that was John McCain's strategy in the 2000 Republican race. Those with a more traditional party appeal focus on caucus states and those with closed primaries; that was the strategy followed by Al Gore in beating Bill Bradley in the Democratic party the same year. Candidates who are identified with a clear ideology often focus on states in which they feel their views will be welcomed and sidestep other states; centrist candidates can appeal more broadly but run the risk of losing to conservative candidates in some states and to liberals in others. Finally, because momentum is so important, because the political calendar is concentrated in the early months of the process, and for

9. President George H. W. Bush waves from the back of the train outside Bowling Green on a whistle-stop campaign trip through Ohio in September 1992.

those accepting public money continued funding is dependent on results in each set of primaries, candidates must find places in which they can succeed among the early primary and caucus states.

In fact, monetary concerns increasingly motivate strategic decision making at the party level as well. The recent trend toward front-loading has to do, in large part, with fund-raising considerations. In fact, for the first time since 1948, the 2016 Republican party convention will be held in July, rather than in August or September. Selecting a nominee earlier allows the party to lengthen the general election season and start spending sooner.

Critiquing the nominating process

In looking at these strategic notions, one is struck by a lack of connection between the variables at play here and those that make either a good president or, with the possible exception of

appeal to independents, a good general election candidate. And therein lies the problem in the nominating process and the cause for criticism.

If one were to design a nominating process from scratch, one would seek a system that resulted in the choice of two candidates who had demonstrated the ability to lead the nation and who showed broad appeal both within the party and to a wider audience. The current system does little to test the ability or even the experience of the nominees; it is skewed in favor of those who do well in Iowa and New Hampshire, two states that are not representative of the nation in demographic terms or in terms of the issues that are most important, and that are not representative of either party, in terms of ideology or their party constituents. Nominees are chosen by relatively few voters (the turnouts in the presidential primaries, even most of the early ones, are quite low and in caucuses even lower), with voters in many states—those selecting convention delegates late in the process—having no influence at all. Finally, because the process is so condensed, because candidates are not tested over an extended period of time on a range of issues, and because most of this occurs well in advance of the time when the average citizen is thinking about presidential politics, citizens are often dissatisfied with one or both of the major party nominees by the time the fall general election campaign begins.

The parties and the media have noted this problem. But solutions are difficult to find. The Republicans, in the prelude to the 2016 nominating process, have discouraged front-loading: States—beyond the four that have regularly held their primaries and caucuses in January and February—that decide to hold their races prior to March 1 stand to lose over half of their delegates. Still, given the national attention devoted to the early nominating contests, it is unlikely that such sanctions will be sufficient to discourage states from continuing to schedule their primaries and caucuses earlier.

The 2016 presidential nominations

Recall figure 5.1. The 2016 presidential nominating contest most clearly reflects that of 2008, when the incumbent was leaving office and when neither party had a presumptive nominee. For the Republicans, Arizona senator John McCain, who had been the runner-up for the 2000 Republican nomination against George W. Bush, was at the top of the field. Despite losing the first contest, the Iowa caucuses, to former Arkansas governor Mike Huckabee, McCain managed to overcome Huckabee and other well-known Republicans, including former Massachusetts governor Mitt Romney and former New York City mayor Rudy Giuliani. By early March, McCain had secured the nomination.

For the Democrats, the nomination process proved to be significantly longer and more competitive. New York senator and former First Lady Hillary Rodham Clinton was the front runner, but after Illinois senator Barack Obama won three out of the four earliest nominating contests, it became clear that Clinton's path to victory was not guaranteed. Over the next few months, Clinton and Obama each won delegates in different states; by the spring, Obama had opened a substantial lead over Clinton in delegates. Yet Clinton continued her campaign, convinced that she could still overtake his delegate count at the August convention by garnering support from "superdelegates"—party leaders and elected officials who serve as delegates at party conventions but who are free to pledge their support to any candidate, as they are not elected in primaries and caucuses. The Democrats would not secure their nominee until after the last primaries in early June, when Obama's delegate count surpassed the 2,118 needed to win the nomination and Clinton conceded the race.

On the eve of the first caucuses in 2016, Hillary Clinton again appeared to be the favorite for the Democratic nomination. Still, as her loss in 2008 proved, her nomination was certainly not set in stone. Vermont senator Bernie Sanders had run a spirited

campaign and led in some early polls, and former Maryland governor Martin O'Malley remained in the race. By contrast, the Republican field appeared to be much more scattered, with prominent Republicans like former Florida governor Jeb Bush, New Jersey governor Chris Christie, Texas senator Ted Cruz, former Arkansas governor Mike Huckabee, Ohio governor John Kasich, Kentucky senator Rand Paul, Florida senator Marco Rubio, and former Pennsylvania senator Rick Santorum still on the ballot as the first contests approached. Outsiders like business magnate Donald Trump, retired neurosurgeon Ben Carson, and former CEO of Hewlett-Packard Carly Fiorina were also running, with Trump emerging as the leader as the voting began. Will ideological splits serve to separate serious contenders from also-rans? Will one of the candidates appealing to the social conservative wing of the party prevail, or will one of the more traditional Republican contenders bar such a fringe candidate from becoming a front runner for the nomination?

The general election campaign

The concern expressed in the late fall of 2000, when the result of the presidential election was still in limbo, was multifaceted. Surely, American citizens—and those viewing the process throughout the world—were concerned because the outcome was in doubt; Americans did not know who the leader of the most powerful nation in the world would be. In part, perhaps this was exacerbated because neither of the two contenders had generated much enthusiasm among the electorate; the world was waiting anxiously to see which of two candidates would become president.

In part, concern was expressed because of the process of the recount. Should the American presidency really be decided by how some unelected judges interpret voter intentions on flawed ballots? No one had heard of a "hanging chad" before November 2000. No one knew who the election officials who were making

these decisions were. In the past, no one cared, but given the tightness of the race, the results were crucial.

The Electoral College

But mostly the concern centered on the process itself, the unique but rarely understood institution of the Electoral College. The average American knows that the Electoral College system exists but not how it works. Americans hold that majority rule is a good thing; few understand that a majority (or even a plurality) of the voters might not elect a president.

The technical workings of the Electoral College are quite simple. Each state is allotted a number of electoral votes equal to the number of representatives it has in the House of Representatives plus the number of senators (two in each case). Each state determines how its electors will be chosen, with the stipulation that no elector may hold any other office of trust under the Constitution. In forty-eight of the fifty states and in the District of Columbia, the electors pledged to the candidates for president and vice president who receive a plurality of the popular votes in the general election are elected and cast their votes accordingly. Presidents like George W. Bush can be elected even though another candidate wins a plurality of the nationwide popular vote if one candidate (e.g., Bush in 2000) wins some of his states by narrow margins (e.g., Florida by 537 votes, New Hampshire by 7,211 votes) while the opponent wins his states roughly comparable in terms of electoral votes by wide margins (Gore, in Rhode Island by 118,953, in Illinois by 569,605 votes).

Alternatives to the Electoral College system

A number of alternatives have been proposed to the Electoral College system. The most obvious alternative would be to switch to a system of direct election of the president, simply counting the votes cast nationwide. Others claim that the best system would be a system in which the slight advantage to the small states given by awarding them electors for their two senators was maintained, but

the electoral votes should be awarded proportionally, reflecting the popular vote in the state. Still others feel that the system in place in Maine and Nebraska, the district plan, should be implemented nationally. Some claim that the system should stay in place, but that the elector votes should be cast automatically, ridding the system of the problem of the faithless elector.

Faithless electors

Nine electors have cast votes for presidential candidates other than the person to whom they were pledged since 1948. Some of these have apparently voted in error, as in the unnamed Kerry elector from Minnesota, who voted for Kerry's running mate, John Edwards, instead, apparently mixing up his "Johns." Others, like D.C.'s Gore delegate, Barbara Lett-Simmons, who left her ballot blank in 2000, and thus broke faith with the electorate, did so purposefully, in her case as a protest of D.C.'s "colonial" status—without representation in Congress.

Numerous variations of each of these alternatives have been proposed. They all reflect dissatisfaction with the system that currently exists and often an estimate of the most radical reform that could be adopted. The direct election of the president most closely resembles the democratic ideal. Whoever receives the most votes wins the election. Just like in most other elections in this country. That sounds simple enough.

But what if three or four major candidates were running for president? Some claim that the Electoral College system, with its winner-take-all feature, especially when combined with single-member district, plurality winners in almost all legislative seats in the country, discourages serious third parties from forming. If the Electoral College system were eliminated, these analysts reason, additional parties might form, and votes might be spread more or less evenly among a number of candidates. Should

someone be elected president with only 30 or 35 percent of the vote? Would it be wise to have a system in which a president is elected with far more than a majority voting against him or her? It is one thing to have legislators, one member in a body of 100 or 435, be elected with only a plurality; it is quite another to choose the leader of the most powerful nation in the world that way.

Some claim that the system should be a direct popular vote, with a runoff if no candidate receives a majority of the votes cast. Others say that there should be a runoff if no candidate receives more than a super plurality, say 45 percent. Those systems would still meet the democratic value of each vote counting, but they would also deal with the problem of minority rulers. Each of these systems might well lead to frequent runoffs in a reconstituted party system. Would that kind of uncertainty be an improvement over the current system, which has had the advantage in nearly all cases of reaching a decisive result in a relatively short time?

These philosophical questions are not easy to resolve, but even if consensus could be reached, political realities argue against a shift to direct election. First, on a very practical level, the kinds of ballot counting issues that appeared in 2000 frighten many politicians. Put simply, they do not trust those in the other party in areas in which their opponents dominate. Stories abound of attempts to steal elections. In 2008, claims of voter fraud emerged when it was found that the Association of Community Organizations for Reform Now (ACORN)—a group that endorsed and worked with the Obama campaign—had submitted fraudulent voter registration forms. Others have expressed concerns about foreign voters, though most claims of voter fraud remain unfounded. These tales may be apocryphal, but they are believed by enough politicians to give pause about going to direct election. Each state's officials feel they can keep tabs on what happens in their area, but they worry about the opportunity for fraud as the electorate expands.

Minority voters are adamantly opposed to reform of the Electoral College system. African Americans and Hispanics each make up approximately 10 percent of the American electorate, but those citizens are not spread evenly throughout the nation. While a 10 percent voting bloc might not get much attention in a national election, if it is concentrated in certain important areas, where it can make the difference between winning a state's electoral votes or losing them, that influence is enhanced.

Finally, some small states would resist change. On the one hand, one could argue that small states have so few electoral votes that no one cares about them. After all, Wyoming and the other of the smallest states have only three electors; even midsized states like Connecticut, Iowa, Oklahoma, or Oregon have only seven; their numerical influence pales compared to the fifty-five for California, thirty-eight for Texas or twenty-nine each for Florida and New York. What difference do the two extra electoral votes that each state automatically receives make when the gap is so large? But, on the other hand, closely contested small states in close elections receive much more attention than they otherwise would. Their representatives want to keep the small advantage that they have.

Strategic considerations because of the Electoral College system

If the average citizen is not aware of the implications of the Electoral College system, every campaign strategist certainly is. Presidential campaigns do not look for every last popular vote; they look for the magic number of electoral votes—270. On election night 2000, as the Florida electoral votes were first thought to be in the Gore column, then the Bush column, then in limbo, television viewers saw how campaign strategists think. Analysts like NBC News Washington bureau chief Tim Russert plotted the course of the election: "If Vice President Gore does not win Florida, then he has to pick up [a variety of combinations of states still too close to call] to reach the magic 270." Those are the calculations campaign managers make.

They start with their base, the states they know they will win or at least that they cannot afford to lose if they are going to win the election. For the Democrats those are the New England states, New York, and California; for the Republicans, the heartland, Bible Belt states, and much of the South. They know that it will take only a minimal effort to secure their base and that no effort, no matter how valiant, will dent the base of the other party. The strategy follows naturally; do not invest many resources in either of these sets of states; the result is essentially predetermined.

Then the real fun begins. Which states are truly "in play"? Which states might you win with a maximum effort? How many electoral votes do they hold? How many of those states must be won to reach the magic 270, a majority of the Electoral College? Of course, the two campaigns are running on parallel tracks. If the Democrats go after New Hampshire, then the Republicans must make a decision—how much is it worth to them to defend that state? If the Republicans make a pitch for West Virginia, how will the Democrats respond? Judgments are checked and rechecked throughout the campaign. Both camps poll in the pivotal states. If the polls are tightening, they invest more resources. If they are pulling away or falling behind, they adjust accordingly.

In the two most recent elections, by early fall the two parties had reached the same conclusions about which states were seen as true contests: the battleground states. In each election, the battle was fought in approximately fourteen states. Closely divided states in one election tend to be closely divided in the next. Colorado, Florida, Indiana, Iowa, Michigan, New Hampshire, North Carolina, Nevada, New Mexico, North Carolina, Ohio, Pennsylvania, Virginia, and Wisconsin were among the battleground states in both 2008 and 2012; these states have 151 electoral votes among them. If one looks at the states in the two parties' bases, the Democrats are about 77 electoral votes short of 270; the Republicans, 90. Each side understands that it needs to

concentrate its effort on these pivotal states and the few others that become competitive in any particular election.

What are the strategic implications of concentrating on such few states? Americans who lived in the battleground states in 2008 and 2012 were overwhelmed by visits to their states by the presidential candidates, their running mates, their wives, and other surrogates. Americans living in the other thirty-six states rarely had campaign visits. Television viewers in the battleground states could hardly turn on their sets without seeing campaign ads sponsored by the two candidates, their parties, or other organizations supporting them. Viewers in other states rarely saw a presidential campaign commercial. Polling data revealed that interest was higher in the battleground states and that voter knowledge of and opinion about the issues and candidates was higher; and on election day, turnout was higher as well.

Were the Electoral College system not in place, candidate strategies would be different. Candidates would concentrate on major media markets, because they could reach most voters in that way. They would concentrate on areas of their strength, because turnout of supporters would be important. Intriguingly, they would not concentrate on states or on areas in which the vote was likely to be close; they would be afraid of drawing their opponent's supporters to the polls. If one won a state by 5,000 votes or lost it by the same margin, it would mean less than attracting an additional 15,000 voters in a state you were already going to win in a landslide.

Is one system better than the other in terms of optimizing the linkage between voters and the government? In a macro sense, no answer is apparent. It is clear that the current system favors those states in which the election is likely to be close; candidates spend time and resources there and, one could argue, incumbent candidates seek support in those states by directing favorable actions their way while in office. It is equally clear that a system with direct election of the president would favor citizens in larger cities—and

such a system would also favor citizens in a state that leaned in the direction of an incumbent's party, because he would curry favor in order to improve turnout. In politics, where one stands on a policy controversy is often determined by where one sits. Reformers will continue to agitate over the Electoral College system, but major reforms in American politics only come on the heels of demonstrated problems that strike the public consciousness. If the 2000 result did not lead to Electoral College reform, it is unlikely that any change is on the horizon.

Funding presidential campaigns

During the 2000 and 2004 presidential campaigns, political journalists and reformers were more concerned about how these races were funded than about how the votes were counted or tabulated. The Federal Election Campaign Act established a system of full public funding for presidential campaigns; the two major parties receive the same amount of money ($74.6 million in 2004); minor parties receive funds in proportion to the vote they received in the previous election, once a minimum threshold of 5 percent of the vote was reached.

After years of demands for reform, the McCain-Feingold bill, the Bipartisan Campaign Reform Act, passed Congress in 2002. National parties were restricted from accepting soft money—money spent on politics but not regulated and largely not reported; to offset this restriction somewhat, hard-money limits were raised. Limits were placed on organizations that mentioned federal candidates in their advertisements. Opponents' arguments that the law unconstitutionally limited free speech rights of those seeking involvement in the process were rejected by the Supreme Court in *McConnell v. Federal Election Commission*, 540 U.S. 93 (2003). Arguments that the reforms would sound the death knell for parties fell on deaf ears.

The 2004 elections were the first run under the limits imposed by BCRA. A number of lessons were quickly learned—or perhaps

relearned for those who had followed campaign finance reform for some time. First, those seeking to influence the political process through spending money will find a way to do so. Political activists found a loophole in the Internal Revenue Service code that allowed them to establish groups—so-called 527 groups, named for the section of the code that described them—that could spend huge sums of money to influence the election. Groups such as the Swift Boat Veterans for Truth, which supported President Bush, and America Coming Together (ACT), which supported Senator Kerry, spent more money in battleground states than either of the two candidates' campaign committees.

Yet in a January 2010 decision, *Citizens United v. Federal Election Commission*, 558 U.S. (2010), the Supreme Court ruled BCRA's prohibition on corporate and union independent expenditures—money spent on behalf of a candidate but not contributed to or in coordination with that candidate—unconstitutional. A decision in the case of *Speechnow.org v. Federal Election Commission* 599 F. 3d (D.C. Cir., Mar. 26, 2010), cert. denied 131 S.Ct. 553 (2010), two months later asserted that such groups could collect unlimited and undisclosed donations. Consequently, the 2012 election revealed massive amounts of outside spending through super PACs—independent expenditure-only groups. In 2012, outside groups, excluding party committees, spent over $1 billion, compared to under $340 million just four years earlier, in 2008. While some have pushed for reform, given the Court's two rulings, significant campaign finance reform limiting such outside spending is unlikely, as it would require a constitutional amendment—an extensive and lengthy process.

Summary: A view toward the 2016 presidential election

What can we know about the 2016 presidential election, some time before the details of the contest have been revealed? What can we

know about the process through which Barack Obama's successor will be chosen?

Perhaps the most obvious point is that little in the process has changed since that much criticized election of 2000. The election will be dominated by the two major national political parties; minor parties or independent candidates will play little or no role.

The nominees of the parties will be chosen through a process that confuses most of the electorate at a time when few citizens are focusing on presidential politics. The timing of the process will be such to guarantee that some states, notably Iowa and New Hampshire, will have influence far disproportional to either the size of their populations or the extent to which those populations are representative of the nation as a whole. The vagaries of the primary and caucus calendar will create a situation in which some additional states have a good deal of influence and others, none at all. Very few citizens will participate in the nominating process, but those who do—not formal leaders of party organizations—will be most influential in choosing the nominees. The ability to raise money will be a critical factor in narrowing each party's field to a small number who will eventually have real shots at the nomination. And finally, if history is any guide at all, the ability to govern will be much less important than will be other factors such as the ability to appeal to the electorate on television or the extent to which the candidate finds the correct nuance in expressing his or her position on controversial and salient issues, a subset often different from issues vital to the national interest. We can also be quite certain that the nominees will be exposed to relentless attacks based on their records in office, their public statements, and perhaps their personal lives and those of their families—and that in at least some cases, these attacks will be unfair, irrelevant, and still decisive.

Once the nominees are chosen and the fall campaign begins in earnest, another set of factors comes into play. The contest will be fought in a relatively small number of states. While the campaigns

10. **Moderator Jim Lehrer and George W. Bush listen to Democratic candidate Al Gore as he answers a question during the presidential debate in Wait Chapel at Wake Forest University in October 2000.**

will each discuss a wide variety of issues, the most important appeals will be on a small number of concerns that divide the candidates—and the voters in battleground states. Debates will be held between the candidates, but we have no guarantee of whether substantive differences between the candidates will be revealed in these debates. However, whether based on substance or style, on overall impression or one reached because of a momentary lapse, the public will form opinions based on these debates.

A great deal of money will be spent in the general election. We know that the two parties will spend tens of millions and that outside groups will again play a major role, collecting unlimited amounts from anonymous individuals, corporations, and unions. In recent years, individual donors have become especially important. Given that wealthy individual donors tend to give to outside groups that often do not disclose their donors, it is difficult to measure their exact contributions, though groups like the Center

for Responsive Politics make estimates. In 2012, wealthy donors, like Jeffrey Katzenberg on the left, gave a reported $2.6 million in PAC donations on behalf of Barack Obama. On the right, donors like Sheldon Adelson gave $20 million in PAC donations on behalf of Newt Gingrich during the primary and another $30 million for Romney during the general election. Such donations can make a substantial impact on the race, at least in the short term; with financial backing from Adelson, Gingrich was able to compete in— and even win—the South Carolina primary; without the support, he likely would have had to suspend his campaign earlier. Still, looking ahead to 2016, we do not know which candidates such donors will support, how much they will spend, and what effect that spending will have.

Finally, we know with some certainty that, at most, slightly over half of the eligible voters will cast a ballot, hardly an overwhelming endorsement considering that on average around 75 percent of the eligible voters exercise the franchise in most modernized democracies, even excluding those with compulsory voting. While citizens in the United States point to their democracy with pride, while the president assiduously works to export American democracy, clearly some aspects of the system fail to reach the ideal to which a truly effective democracy should strive.

Chapter 6
Subnational nominations and elections

In April 2014, more than six months before the national elections, David Wasserman of the *Cook Political Report* projected sure winners in 357 of the 435 races for the House of Representatives; he was right on all of them. He felt that "likely" winners were apparent in an additional thirty-four seats and that thirty other seats "leaned" one way or the other; his early judgment was altered by campaigns or events in only two of those sixty-four seats. Months before the average citizen began to focus on upcoming elections, Wasserman correctly identified winners in 421 of the 435 House races. Only fourteen districts featured races that Wasserman felt were too competitive to identify a favorite in— again, six months before the votes were cast.

Few Americans know how little electoral competition exists in their vaunted democracy. Elections to the House of Representatives stand as a stark example. By almost any measure— incumbents defeated, margins of victory, number of uncontested elections—the 2006 and 2008 congressional elections were among the least competitive in history. One had to go back more than a decade to find an election in which fewer than 98 percent of the House incumbents seeking reelection have done so successfully. Even in the Republican sweep in 2010, approximately 85 percent of the incumbents seeking reelection were successful in their

campaigns. More than 90 percent of the races in the last twenty years have been won by margins of more than 10 percent; in 2014, only 26 of the 435 House races were decided by less than 5 percent of the vote, 318 were decided by margins of greater than 20 percent. In the average congressional election, between 10 and 15 percent of the 435 "races" are uncontested. One might think that primary elections provided competition in districts with a strong partisan bias, but over 70 percent of the incumbents seeking reelection faced no primary opposition.

How are candidates selected to run for office below the level of the presidency, and how do they run their general election campaigns? What are the implications of the system of single-member districts with plurality winners used in virtually all American elections, of the ways in which electoral districts are drawn, of the way in which elections are financed, and of the ways in which campaigns are contested?

Most examples will be drawn from elections to the U.S. House of Representatives. As a general rule, nominations and elections for state governor and U.S. senator are more competitive than those for the House; contests for state legislature and local office, less competitive. The general principles are that the more the nomination is worth (in terms of likelihood of subsequent election), the more it is likely to be contested or even hotly contested, and the more influence that an office has, and the less dominated by one party a district is, the more likely one is to find competition in the general election.

The nominating process

When Connecticut senator Joseph Lieberman lost the Democratic nomination to seek reelection in August 2006, casual observers were surprised and confused. How could he have won the convention nomination but then lost a primary? However, as should

surprise no reader of this book by this time, the variations within that norm provide for significant differences among the states.

The formal nominating process for the Democratic and Republican parties is quite simple to understand. The norm is for there to be a primary election in which the party selects its nominee. But state nominating processes vary in:

- Who may vote
- Who may run
- What role the party organizations play in the process
- How much competition is likely
- What it takes to win the nomination.

Who may vote

As with presidential nominations, the question revolves around the role of party membership and whether elections are open to all voters or closed, meaning that only party members may vote. The definitions of party members are crucial here. Nowhere in the United States does the term "party member," as used for the purposes of determining who may vote, refer to formal, dues-paying members. That concept of choosing to be a member of a party is alien to most Americans. Even within this looser conception of party, important variations remain.

Some states (e.g., Connecticut, Oklahoma, and Nevada) have formal processes for enrollment in a party, party lists maintained by public officials, public access to party membership, and restrictions prohibiting changing party affiliation after the filing date for candidates for office. Another group of states (e.g., Massachusetts, South Dakota, and Arizona) have formal enrollment processes but are more flexible regarding when a voter can change party registration, with some (such as Ohio) allowing switches on primary voting day. These states also vary in terms of whether and when they allow those not enrolled in a party to enroll in one of the

parties for the purpose of voting in primary elections. Finally, another group of states (e.g., Tennessee, Illinois, and Missouri) require voters to declare party affiliation on primary day, but no public record is kept of these choices. In all, thirty-nine states have some form of closed primary, although the variations noted above show how misleading this classification can be.

A very thin line separates the last group of closed primary states from the open primary states (e.g., Vermont, Wisconsin, and Hawaii), meaning those states that permit voters to choose among party ballots within the secrecy of the voting booth.

Washington State passed a ballot initiative instituting a "top two" primary. In these contests, all candidates in a given race are on the ballot, and the first- and second-place candidates advance to the general election, regardless of their party affiliation. Thus, two members of the same party could end up competing in the general election.

In 2006, in the case of *Washington State Republican Party v. Washington*, 460 F.3d 1108 (9th Cir. 2006), the U.S. Court of Appeals for the Ninth District upheld a lower court decision, declaring the initiative unconstitutional. However, the Supreme Court in *Washington State Grange v. Washington State Republican Party, et al.*, 552 U.S. 442 (2008), reversed the lower courts' decisions, arguing that the top-two primary did not, in fact, "impose a severe burden on the political parties' associational rights." In 2012, Washington implemented the top-two primary in all elections except presidential elections.

The importance of who may vote is strategic. Party leaders feel that a closed system is more likely to lead to more loyal followers of the party platform as the nominee than is an open system. The Democratic, Republican, and Libertarian parties in Washington came together to oppose the top-two primary, demonstrating how

this ultimate step toward opening the system undermined efforts at party unity.

Who may run

States vary on two questions with regard to who may run in a party's primary. The more basic question involves party membership: states differ in how they define the allegiance a prospective candidate must have demonstrated to a party. The principle is clear—Republicans run for the Republican nomination, and Democrats for the Democratic nomination.

The second issue concerns how one qualifies for the ballot. In a few states political party committees control or at least can grant access to the ballot. In most states, however, candidates get on the ballot through obtaining signatures on a nominating petition. The important questions relate to who may sign the petitions and how many signatures are required. More difficult requirements—large numbers of signatures, only from party members, dispersed geographically throughout the constituency—mean that only candidates with their own well-developed political organization or candidates backed by an existing organization, like the political party, can get on the ballot. Easier requirements—relatively few signatures, from anyone, living anywhere—make it easier for amateur candidates to run in a primary. More difficult petition requirements or an increased role for the party organization means that more traditional candidates are likely to run.

A quick reaction is that easier requirements are more democratic; after all, no one is kept off of the ballot by bureaucratic restrictions. And many support that view. However, if *anyone* can run for office, many people often do just that. If many names appear on the ballot for the same office, the electorate can have a difficult time distinguishing among them—and separating those who have a serious chance from more frivolous candidates. Because elections are often determined by plurality vote, a crowded field often means a winner with relatively little

support. Relatively unsuccessful candidates might draw votes disproportionately from a losing serious candidate, thus affecting the primary outcome. Is that indeed more democratic?

The role of party organization in the nominating process

As noted earlier, one of the basic roles of a political party is to guarantee that electoral contests exist. Political parties recruit candidates for office. But should they be able to determine which candidate runs under their label if more than one candidate chooses to do so? If party leaders recruit a candidate, should they have the power (or the authority) to "de-recruit" others seeking the nomination? If party leaders think one candidate has a much better chance of winning the general election than another, should they be able to campaign actively—either personally or as an organization—for their preferred candidate?

Those who favor strong political parties and see them as central to an effectively functioning democracy would answer those questions affirmatively. Those who think that political parties corrupt the democratic process would answer them in the negative. Party history in the various states has varied tremendously; that is why some states have closed party systems and some are more open. Similarly, the historical strength of party organizations in various states has determined the modern role that they play in the nominating process.

At one extreme are the states in which parties play an important or even a determining role in nominations. In Utah, if a candidate receives 70 percent of the vote at a state party's convention, that candidate is nominated; if no one receives the 70 percent, the primary is held between the top two finishers at the convention. In Connecticut, for many offices, the party choice is the nominee unless she or he is challenged by someone else, either a candidate receiving 20 percent of the convention or caucus vote, or a candidate filing a petition with a significant number of signatures. That is how Ned Lamont, who beat Joe Lieberman, got on the

ballot; Lieberman won the convention endorsement but lost the primary election. Such successful challenges are rare. Indeed, since 1996, in Connecticut, fewer than 10 percent of the party-endorsed candidates for Congress have faced any primary at all. In other states, the candidate winning the party convention is guaranteed a spot on the primary ballot (and in some cases the top spot), while other candidates must file petitions.

An intermediate position in terms of the role of party is found in states in which party does not play a formal role in the process but rather plays an informal yet still influential role. The quintessential example of this would be influence of the Cook County Democratic Party in Chicago, Illinois. The endorsement of the Daley organization, run by two generations of mayors of Chicago, has been tantamount to nomination for nearly half a century, except for brief flurries of activity by reform elements. Recently the Arizona Democratic Party has experimented with a new type of influence, certifying candidates, at times more than one in the same race, whom they perceive to be credible in the general election—and by implication de-certifying those who do not receive their approval.

At the other extreme in terms of party influence are those states that are prohibited from choosing among primary candidates. In some states, party rules prohibit the organization from choosing among candidates; in others, party officers as well as the organization must stay neutral. Party officials in these states can find themselves in a difficult position. If they recruit a candidate and that candidate then draws an opponent, they cannot assist the candidate they encouraged to run. However, if they do not recruit a candidate, and no one chooses to run for a particular office, they have failed to do their job appropriately.

The amount of competition

Not surprisingly, competition for party nominations varies tremendously around the country. The variables that determine

whether or not there will be primary competition are easily identified: partisanship of the district; importance of the office; presence or absence of a strong incumbent; and strength of the party organization.

In heavily Republican areas, the GOP (Grand Old Party) nomination is more valued (because it is more likely to lead to victory in the general election) and more competition ensues. But the Democratic nominations in those areas are less frequently contested. The opposite, of course, is true in heavily Democratic areas. Nominations for local office and state legislature are more likely to be awarded without contest than those for governor or U.S. senator. In fact, for the more local offices, the role of party is often to find someone who will run and serve if elected. If a powerful incumbent is seeking reelection, competition in his or her party is extremely unlikely, and competition in the other party is quite unlikely. Finally, strong party organizations normally fill the ballot and discourage challenges to their candidates; weaker party organizations are more likely to have ballot positions unfilled and competition for the more valued positions.

As noted above, 70 percent of all incumbents running for reelection to the House of Representatives have been renominated without opposition in recent years. Very few of the others have faced serious challenges. And, except in the years following redistricting (when two incumbents might be placed in the same district), very few lose nomination challenges—fewer than five in every cycle except those immediately after redistricting for the last three decades. Competition for nominations to oppose incumbents is more common; the most likely context in which primaries will be contested is for open seats, particularly in a party that dominates a district. In those cases winning the nomination is more likely to lead to success in the general election.

Who wins the nomination

In the vast majority of states, primary winners are determined by plurality rule, the candidate with the most votes wins. Clearly, this rule is nonproblematic in uncontested primaries or in those with only two candidates running. However, in states with low ballot-access thresholds, valuable nominations are often contested by more than two candidates. In those cases, nomination by plurality can result in the general election candidacy of a candidate who would not have been the choice of the majority.

Nine states require a majority of the vote for nomination, with runoffs between the top two finishers if no one achieves a majority on the first vote. Runoff primaries were instituted in the South during the period when only the Democratic candidates had any chance in the general election. Essentially the primaries determined the winner. In the modern era, with Republicans dominant in many regions in the South, some African American politicians claim that runoff primaries work against their interest; the argument was put forth with great rhetorical flourish by Jesse Jackson two decades ago, citing one notable example. However, the historical experience has shown that the runoff assures a candidate with widespread support and has not had a deleterious effect on the candidacy of African Americans over time.

A pragmatic view of the nominating process

While it is important to understand the nominating process and how variations in the process lead to different results, it is also important not to lose the forest for the trees. Except for nominations for open seats—for important offices in a party whose candidates have a legitimate chance of winning—very few primaries in the United States are hotly contested. In most cases only one candidate seeks a party's nomination for an office. Some of those candidates are self-starters; others are recruited by party leaders.

In all too many cases, if one espouses basic democratic values, no one comes forth to run, and party leaders are generally unsuccessful at recruiting candidates. In those cases, if an incumbent is seeking reelection, he or she serves another term without the electorate making any evaluation of previous service. If no incumbent is running, the electorate is faced with no choice as to who will govern. While it is rare for a governor or a U.S. senator to be elected or reelected without any opposition, it happens with alarming regularity for other offices—about 15 percent of the time for U.S. House races in recent years; an average of more than 30 percent of the time for state legislative races.

Nominations go begging for a variety of reasons. First and foremost is that potential candidates do not think that they can win because of such factors as the power of incumbency, partisan redistricting, and the cost of elections. We will address these factors in the following section on general elections. Beyond that, potential candidates do not emerge because parties are often too weak to provide enough encouragement. When party organizations identify strong potential candidates and encourage them to run, they often do so. Strong potential candidates who do not run have said that lack of an effective party support network is one deterrent. In addition, strong potential candidates do not run because they simply are not interested in campaigning or serving—because they prefer the position they currently hold, because they do not like the process of running, because they feel that the personal and professional costs of service would exceed the personal and professional gains, or for a combination of these reasons.

General elections

The reason to study how elections function is to determine if they contribute to effective democracy. Studies of voting behavior in the United States focus on presidential voting; while analysts

differ in their interpretations, a consensus has emerged that party affiliation and an evaluation of the performance of the president are important factors in determining how citizens vote. One could argue that reliance on evaluations of factors such as those is consistent with democratic values. Does the same hold true for elections below the level of the presidency?

Gubernatorial and senatorial elections

Dividing subnational elections between those for more and less salient offices is useful. The news media—and thus the public—concentrate on a few, highly visible elections. Campaigns in many of these races are fiercely fought and tightly contested. Most other races, however, feature little campaigning and much less electoral competition.

At the state level, gubernatorial elections, held in nonpresidential election years in forty-one states, gain the most attention. In 2014 thirty-six governorships were on the ballot. In twenty-eight of those cases, incumbents sought reelection; all of them faced challengers. Most of the challengers were serious candidates, able to raise money and take their campaign message to the public. Fifteen of the incumbents were involved in hard-fought campaigns, against opponents with impressive political credentials and campaign war chests that guaranteed extensive media campaigns—U.S. representatives, former governors who had given up office earlier because of term limits, statewide elected officials.

Eight other gubernatorial races were in open seats, three vacated by incumbents not choosing to seek reelection, one by an incumbent defeated in a primary, and four by incumbents prohibited from doing so because of term limits. Seven of those eight races were competitive, with strong candidates running for each party. Throughout the fall, each campaign worked to get its message to the electorate, messages based on evaluations of the previous incumbent and promises for the years ahead. Open seat

races tend to be competitive, with the electorate presented with a meaningful choice. Three governorships changed party hands in 2014.

Gubernatorial races tend to be decided on state issues; citizens evaluate their governors as executives and judge how well they have run the state since the last election. Elections to the U.S. Senate tend to focus on national issues. In 2014 thirty-six states held elections for one of their seats in the U.S. Senate. Because Democratic political fortunes were waning nationally as the election year approached, Republicans hoped to recapture partisan control of the body. Before the beginning of the election year, seven senators (five Democrats and two Republicans) announced their retirements. Of the twenty-nine incumbents seeking reelection, months before the election sixteen appeared to be totally secure, and all sixteen of those incumbents won. Intense competition was found in two of the open seats and in six of the seats held by incumbents (five by Democrats and one by a Republican). Literally millions of dollars were poured into these races. The candidates for both parties in the open seats and challenging the incumbents in the others were experienced politicians, with many surrendering other important positions to run for the Senate. In November a quarter of the contested seats changed party hands as the Republicans reclaimed the majority.

What can one conclude about these elections for important public office? First, in many cases, strong candidates were nominated in both parties, they received substantial financial backing, and they ran aggressive campaigns. Citizens casting votes in those races had the opportunity to be informed and to choose who should represent them on a rational basis. This kind of effective campaigning was evident in the 2014 elections in about thirty states, in races either for governor or for U.S. senator or for both.

However, in the other twenty states, including four that had contests for both offices, incumbents were reelected without

serious competition. One might think that this lack of competition was caused by a strong partisan bias in the state; that in fact was the case in heavily Democratic New York, where Governor Andrew Cuomo and Senator Kirsten Gillibrand were each reelected easily. But it was not the case in other states, as in Maryland, with a Republican governor and Democratic senators. In these cases the power of incumbency and personal organization, not partisanship, deterred potentially strong candidates. And, in these cases, citizens dissatisfied with performance had little opportunity for effective opposition.

Congressional and state legislative elections

Fair Vote—the Center for Voting and Democracy is a reform-minded nongovernmental organization (NGO) with the goal of improving voter turnout and fair elections. Active since 1992, the group has focused a good deal of attention on races for the House of Representatives, the branch of American government designed by the founding generation to be closest to the people. Fair Vote's report on House elections is aptly named "Dubious Democracy."

Little competition exists for House seats. In election after election over the past three decades, with the sole exception of that in 2010, over 90 percent of the incumbents seeking reelection have done so successfully. Few of those face serious opposition; many face no opponent at all—in the primary or in the general election. Potentially strong candidates who might be interested in running for the House typically wait for a seat to become open before they enter a race. As a result, incumbents face weaker candidates who do not have the ability to raise money and thus cannot carry their message to the electorate.

Why are incumbents seemingly invulnerable? Many factors contribute to incumbent safety: their ability to ingratiate themselves to their constituents, largely through perquisites available to all House members; their ability to raise money,

particularly from interest groups whose positions they favor; the skill of those who draw district lines to favor one party or the other; and personal organizations and campaign skills, honed in the first successful race for the House and refined in each subsequent election.

Are high incumbent reelection rates a problem—recognizing that state legislators are reelected at rates as high as congressmen, with many fewer facing any opposition at all? Some argue that if citizens cared enough about replacing an incumbent, they would do so. After all, in 1994 the Republicans gained control of the House after decades of Democratic rule, beating thirty-four Democratic incumbents and picking up a total of fifty-four seats. In 2006 enough seats switched hands for control to go back to the Democrats, and then in 2010 the Republicans regained the majority.

Those counterexamples are important but must be examined with perspective. American democracy is based on the premise that citizens should have the ability to express their support for or opposition to the policies of the government at frequent intervals. While the appearance of democracy remains intact, exercising that right is difficult. That conclusion holds whether one looks at the district level or at the national level.

In 2006 Republicans in Congress were reeling under a series of scandals; majority leader Tom DeLay resigned his post while under indictment in his home state of Texas, and he and many of his GOP colleagues were caught in the web of super-lobbyist Jack Abramoff's illegal schemes and payoffs.

After the slim passage of the Affordable Care Act in 2010, Democratic president Barack Obama's popularity sank; House Republicans capitalized on the opportunity in order to please the public, voting over fifty times to repeal the act between 2010 and 2014, though this move was simply symbolic, because such a

measure would not pass the Democratic Senate. Still, Republicans had to scramble to find enough districts that were competitive.

The key question in analyzing an election in which one party has a distinct advantage nationally is whether that party has enough strong candidates to convert some seats (seemingly safe for their opponents) to competitive status. In 2012, Republicans did this handily, maintaining their overwhelming advantage in the House, which had come about in the 2010 midterm elections. In 2014, they did this again, winning an additional twelve seats in the House, and nine in the Senate, giving them control over both chambers. In the final chapter we will return to examine the aspects of the system that restrict the ability of the electorate to voice its opinion.

The quality of campaigns

Democratic theorists agree on basic tenets of fair and effective elections—that opposition parties can challenge those in power, that candidates have the right freely to express their views, that a free press can report on the electoral process, that citizens have the right to vote in secret and without fear, and that voters have access to information needed to cast their votes in an informed manner.

Less agreement exists on how much information is necessary for the electoral process to serve a democracy adequately. Must the electorate be truly informed, know the details of policy alternatives and the candidates' views on those alternatives, in order to vote rationally? Or is it adequate for voters simply to know if they feel comfortable with those in power, in the terms of the question posed so cogently by then-candidate Ronald Reagan in his debate with President Jimmy Carter, "Are you better off now than you were four years ago?" Citizens come by the second kind of knowledge intuitively; they do not need to gather new information in order to vote. Further, given the spread of

the Internet, no one doubts that enterprising, concerned citizens can find the kind of information required to meet the first test. But few citizens are that enterprising or that concerned.

The question then becomes whether, in the few elections that are competitive today, an adequate amount of pertinent information reaches the average citizen through political campaigns and media outlets. Critics claim that it does not. Candidates avoid substance at any cost, because every stand that one takes on a controversial issue makes as many enemies as it does friends. The most effective techniques developed by political consultants involve negative campaigning: control of the agenda by focusing on issues or personal matters that are difficult for your opponent.

Most citizens receive their political information from television; television journalists rarely focus on substantive policies in the small amount of coverage that they give any nonpresidential campaign. The coverage of local campaigns, even the most competitive ones, is often so slight as to be meaningless. Newspapers do a somewhat better job, but they too rarely concentrate on state and local campaigning. When the media do cover campaigns, they tend to focus on who is ahead and what strategy is being followed, not on policy differences between the candidates or differences in candidate qualifications.

The candidate campaigns and the media do not deserve all of the blame for this circumstance. Nor do the citizens, although clearly citizen involvement could be much higher. Citizens are asked to focus on a large number of campaigns at one time (see table 1.1, p. 7). They are busy with their everyday lives; politics, in general, is not central to their existence. And perhaps most important, they do not often see how their lives will be impacted by the election of one person or another, certainly not a congressman or a state legislator. So they pay scant attention to campaigns, focus on them only at the last minute, vote for party or for a candidate with whom

they are familiar, or for those who seem to have or seem not to have improved their sense of well-being.

The media are asked to cover the same number of campaigns. How can they adequately do so? And who will watch? Their resources are limited, and viewer interest is low. Certainly campaign coverage as a public service is part of the responsibility of mass-media outlets, but few go beyond the minimum that is required, especially at calculable economic costs.

And candidates seek to win. Candidates and their consultants do not run negative campaigns because they are inherently bad people. They do so because experience has proven such campaigns to be successful. Clever commercials capture public attention more than do talking heads. A fine line separates comparative advertisements that contrast a candidate's record or policy preference with that of his or her opponent from negative advertisements that attack an opponent unfairly. Often the location of that line is in the eye of the beholder. What one campaign sees as a humorous comparative ad, critical to be sure but within bounds, the other sees as over the line. In the final analysis, citizens judge—and campaign consultants are clear that the citizen test, not that of campaign critics, is the *only* one they monitor.

If none of the participants is to blame for the lack of substance in American campaigns, where does the blame lie? In part, it is inherent in the system. The American system, with single-member districts, weak parties, separated governmental institutions, and a strong federal system, leads almost inevitably to campaigns based on image and not substance. Citizens can know their representatives, but they cannot hold them accountable, because power is dispersed. Parties can take stands on issues, but individual candidates can ignore those positions at their will, because it is their constituents, not national or even state party leaders, who control their destinies.

Summary

Two factors are at work in determining the results of elections below the level of the presidency. On the one hand, analysts look at national trends. How is the party in power viewed by the electorate? Which party does the electorate feel is better able to handle the most salient issues? Is the president popular? Do citizens feel that the country is headed in the right direction? If the electorate is satisfied with the country's direction, supportive of the president, and comfortable with the party in power, little will change as the result of an election. The status quo will be maintained, and that will be an accurate reflection of popular will. If voters are not satisfied with the direction the country is heading, unhappy with presidential performance, and restless about the party in power, democratic theory holds that they should be able to replace those in power with others, who presumably will respond to their desires. That essentially is what happened in the election of 1994, when the Republicans replaced the Democrats as the majority party in the Congress, in 2006, when the Democrats regained control, and in 2010, when the Republicans won again.

On the other hand, analysts are aware of an old adage, often attributed to former Speaker of the House Thomas P. "Tip" O'Neill from Massachusetts: "All politics is local." Those in office serve the day-to-day needs of their constituents, often in ways quite detached from national politics. As a result, incumbent officeholders are most often viewed favorably by those they represent. Those favorable impressions, combined with the considerable electoral assets that an incumbent can amass, make it very difficult to unseat incumbents, even incumbents of an unpopular party. Potential challengers recognize that they start at a distinct disadvantage. Thus, political parties struggle to find quality challengers.

Any evaluation of the American electoral process must deal with the paradox that local representatives of the party in power are viewed favorably by the same voters who view that party unfavorably at the national (or state) level. Popular will at the macro level cannot be expressed if citizens' votes in local elections do not reflect their views on national or state issues at the polls. In American democracy, the role of political parties is to assure that they recruit challengers to incumbents and candidates in open seats who can run campaigns that allow strong national trends to be expressed in local elections. Most state and local elections in the United States are not competitive. For American democracy to function effectively, the parties' task is to assure that enough elections are competitive so that the national or state result can reflect popular will.

Chapter 7

Far from the perfect democracy

Americans, even those familiar with the details of the electoral process, remain convinced that American democracy represents the ideal toward which others should strive. They point to the flaws in other systems—to the split between the president and the prime minister in a country like France, with a mixed system; to the messiness in forming a working majority in a country with a parliamentary system like Israel; to the instability of governments in a country like Italy; to the lack of a free press and an open process in polities once totalitarian but now self-proclaimed democracies like Russia; to racial, gender, or class domination in other countries like India. But Americans rarely turn the spotlight of criticism on their own regime. Five issues—the level of participation, the apparent irrationality governing the presidential nomination and election processes, the cost of American democracy, the lack of competitive elections at many levels in the United States, and the acerbic discourse that characterizes American elections—are of continuing concern. Until public officials in the United States can address these issues, American democracy will continue to fall far short of the ultimate model.

Level of participation

In the Israeli election of March 2015, approximately 72 percent of the voting-age population cast their ballots; that was higher than

in recent Israeli elections but not the level officials had hoped. In November 2008, when just over 62 percent of the eligible citizens of voting age cast their votes for president of the United States, the turnout was the highest in forty-four years and only the sixth time three-fifths of those eligible had voted for president since women were enfranchised in 1920; turnout went down in 2012, and the 36 percent of the eligible voters who cast ballots in the off-year congressional elections represented the lowest turnout in over seventy years; in off-year elections in which state governors are elected in thirty-six states, turnout has never reached 50 percent nationally. The United States falls in the bottom quintile of democracies sorted by turnout.

The concern is not just that Americans vote in lower numbers than do citizens of other democracies. The more serious problem is that those who do vote differ from those who do not in systematic ways. African Americans and Hispanics vote in lower numbers than do Caucasians. Poor people vote in lower numbers than do rich people. Less educated people vote in lower numbers than do those with more education. The chorus of the electorate, in short, sings with a distinctively privileged voice. In a representative democracy, one must worry if policies reflect the desires of the electorate more than those who do not vote. That the privileged vote more is the problem.

Why is turnout low in the United States? Both the American system of government and specific election laws depress turnout. Scholars have known for some time that electoral systems with proportional representation (PR) have higher turnouts than those with first-past-the-post, plurality winners. On average democracies with PR systems have voter turnout 15 percent higher than those with plurality winners. Mixed systems fall somewhere in between.

Even within the electoral system established by the founders, election laws discourage participation in elections. The following merit consideration:

- *Registration laws.* Only 72 percent of those eligible to vote were registered for the 2012 election; only 58 percent of those between eighteen and twenty-four years old. Should registration laws be eased to increase participation?

- *Frequency of elections.* Americans are asked to go to the polls more often than citizens of other nations, because each geographic area sets its own rules and seeks to keep its elections out from under the influence of national trends. As a result, Americans suffer from voting fatigue. Should all elections within the country be held at one time, once a year?

- *Election Day.* All of that voting occurs during the workweek; citizens must fit voting into their already busy schedules. Should Election Day be a holiday as it is in many other nations?

- *Voting as an obligation, not a right.* Voting is not compulsory in the United States, unlike in thirty-two other democracies in which voting is mandatory. Would a change in this factor increase turnout? Would its benefits outweigh the costs?

- *How to count votes.* Related to these questions is the theoretical question of whether the first-past-the-post system is the most democratic, if it most accurately reflects the views of the voters. Does an Instant Runoff System guarantee that the results of an election more accurately reflect the desires of those voting than any other system? If so, would the citizens accept such a change?

Similar arguments are made when any of these changes in the American system are discussed. Some claim that those interested enough in voting have ample opportunity to do so; others assert that the low turnout rate in the United States is a sign of democratic malady. Behind each argument is a political one: who would gain and who would lose if more citizens voted? The question of whether reforms such as these would improve American democracy is clearly secondary to judgments over its political consequences in the minds of those making the decisions.

The presidential nominating and election processes

In the 2012 presidential election, the citizens of the United States were faced with a choice between two candidates they did not much like. Some claim that the voter turnout, much lower than four years earlier, was a reflection of the citizens' responses to the choices offered. President Obama, who had inspired voters in 2008, was seen as incredibly smart but uncomfortably stiff; he had failed to create the change he had promised or to lead the nation out of recession. Republican Mitt Romney was viewed as smart and successful in business, but out of touch with average Americans. Faced with those choices, many voters stayed home.

Certainly that explanation is an oversimplification of the dynamics of the 2012 election, but just as surely observers were left questioning how a great nation with over 300 million people could end up with two such candidates as the only contenders for president. The choice was the result of a flawed nominating process that no one defends. The general election was equally unsatisfactory. Again, obvious issues for students of democracy are in evidence.

- *The influence of Iowa and New Hampshire on presidential nominations.* Iowa and New Hampshire, two states not even remotely representative of followers of either party or of the nation as a whole, dominate the process. Can the influence of these states be reduced while preserving some room for the person-to-person politics they permit?

- *Front-loading of the process.* Similarly most agree that the process is too front-loaded, in that citizens are asked to select a candidate for president before the issues are clear, before they are focusing on the upcoming election. The current process benefits a candidate who has established name recognition, can raise money before the first votes are cast, appeals to the base of his or her party, campaigns well in a one-on-one setting, and has the ability to establish a nationwide organization. Those are not necessarily the qualities

that make the best candidate for a general election in which a candidate must appeal to independents and weak supporters of the other party, have detailed knowledge of the issues of the day and skill in debating those issues in various formats, and a bearing that says to the voters "I am ready to be the leader of the free world." Is there a more rational way to structure the nominating process, a means that will lead to more acceptable candidates?

- *The relationship between candidacy and governing.* The skill sets needed to be a successful president—the ability to work with leaders of both parties, familiarity with world events and the capacity to negotiate with world leaders, a vision of the country's future and of a path to reach that vision, the experience to administer a huge bureaucracy effectively without becoming bogged down in details, the gift to speak to the nation and for the nation with equal effectiveness—are qualities that are best judged by peers, not by mass audiences in an election. But in the American political system, professional peers have little to say about who is nominated and less about who is elected. Is there a way to alter the system so that democratic choices are tempered by peer review?

- *Counting the votes.* The process of election itself has come under severe criticism. The reasons the Electoral College was adopted in 1789 hardly pertain today, but the system has resisted change. Should the Electoral College system be scrapped in favor of one more transparently democratic?

The cost of democracy

What should it cost to run an election? Who should bear that cost? Should the ability to raise money be a factor—or even a determining factor—in who wins an election?

As recently as 1976, the first election after the major reform of the system through which federal campaigns are financed in the United States, the best estimate held that the total amount spent on all elections—federal, state, and local—was $500,000,000.

Prior to the 2008 nominating contests, political consultants estimated that the "cost of entry" into the two parties' presidential nomination races would be $100,000,000 per candidate. For the 2016 race, Hillary Clinton raised $45 million before July 2015; others feared they could not raise enough money to compete.

In the 2014 elections for the U.S. House of Representatives, incumbents seeking reelection outspent their challengers, on the average, by 6 to 1, on average outspending challengers $1.5 million to $225.00. Incumbents facing serious challengers spent much more than that; few than 40 percent of challengers spent even $100,000. The few challengers who beat incumbents were able to spend nearly as much or more than the incumbent.

Campaign finance has long been a concern of political reformers. The first campaign finance legislation was passed over a century ago, when the Tillman Act regulated the contributions of corporations and banks to election campaigns. The most recent reform legislation—the Bipartisan Campaign Reform Act (BCRA) of 2002, popularly known as the McCain-Feingold Act—took years to pass, and then was largely eviscerated by the Supreme Court.

A consensus holds that the campaign finance system is broken. But no consensus exists as to how to fix it, a problem familiar to political reformers. The reason is simple. A reform that helps one group hurts another. Those who are advantaged under one set of rules are disadvantaged under another.

We can briefly explore the basic issues:

- *The cost of campaigns.* Some hold that campaigns cost too much. Others note that Americans spend less on campaign advertising than they do on automobile advertising. Which is more important for the American way of life?

- *Who gives money to campaigns?* Some hold that giving large amounts of money to campaigns is merely another way to influence

outcomes and eventually legislation. Others contend that donating money is not evil, but rather a way to express one's political preferences that should be protected, so long as it is not done in secret. Still others feel that the cost of campaigns should be borne by all citizens equally. Is there a more democratic way to fund electioneering, and, if so, at what level?

- *Disclosure of campaign contributions.* Everyone seems to agree that contributions to campaigns should be made openly and publicly. Some believe that the current system of filing federal or state officials is sufficient. Others maintain that more disclosure and more prompt disclosure are necessary. Is there an appropriate balance between shining a light on those financing campaigns and violating individuals' rights to participate in the process without public disclosure?

- *Who should be regulated?* All involved agree that candidates for office and their campaigns should be regulated. The BCRA also regulated soft-money expenditures, restricting the amount of money that could be given to the parties for more general activities, not related to a specific campaign. However, the Supreme Court has ruled that spending money for political purposes is the equivalent of political speech—and is thus protected by the Constitution. Reformers search for a way to restrict spending without running afoul of the Court. Is there a way to strike a balance, allowing for free political speech but not domination by the wealthy few? How should political speech be regulated without stifling free expression of political beliefs?

The political parties spend an enormous amount of time and effort raising money for their candidates and assisting candidates in raising money for their own campaigns. The key question in the area of campaign finance reform remains unanswered. Can a system be devised that allows enough money to be raised and spent so that campaigns can reach the voters without, at the same time, unfairly advantaging some candidates over others and therefore stifling competition? Can it be done while remaining cognizant of

the political freedoms ensured in the First Amendment to the Constitution?

Lack of competition

The basic premise of a democracy is that those in power can be turned out if the citizenry disapproves of their actions. Competition is necessary. How one defines competition is less than clear, however.

In one sense the electoral system in the United States is extremely competitive. It is hard to imagine an election closer than the presidential election of 2000. Even in 2012, Mitt Romney thought he might win the election, right up until the returns came in after the polls closed. Partisan control of the U.S. House and Senate has been determined by the swing of a few key races in recent elections. Much the same can be said for many state legislatures. Looked at from the perspective of overall partisan control, the electoral system is extremely competitive.

However, if one looks at the state and district levels, much less competition exists. Only about fourteen states have really been in play in the last two presidential elections. In the other thirty-six states, the result was all but known well in advance. Citizens in those states had virtually no opportunity to weigh the candidates or to express their views.

The 2002 and 2004 elections to the House of Representatives were by most accounts the least competitive in modern history. Whether one looks at the reelection rates of incumbents (more than 98 percent in each case), contests in which the loser seriously threatened the winner (about 10 percent in each of those elections), seats in which one party or the other did not even field a candidate or fielded a candidate who polled less than 20 percent of the vote (about three in ten), or the average margin of victory

(about 40 percent), true competition was all but absent. Even in the slightly more competitive recent elections, the vast majority of districts saw little real competition. Results in most state legislative races were similar. Statewide elections—for governor or U.S. senator—were competitive in some states but in others lacked close races as well.

- *Incumbent advantage.* Certainly incumbents have enormous advantages in terms of name recognition, the ability to serve their constituents and to reinforce positive images, experience in campaigning, and ease of fund-raising. But perhaps incumbents have earned those advantages. They have won office initially, after all, and that is no easy task. One could argue that they stay in office and win easily because they are good at what they do. Should the system be altered to reduce the advantages incumbents have or to increase campaign resources for challengers?

- *Redistricting.* For legislative districts, the ways in which district lines are drawn often favors incumbents. Gerrymandering, drawing district lines for political purposes, is as old as the nation and done with increased sophistication and effectiveness today. Creative mapping, however, does not explain one-party states or one-party dominance in some regions. Some scholars claim that those who draw the lines are blamed unfairly for the lack of competition, that citizens tend to congregate into geographic areas with those who share similar views, or that views change to conform with one's neighbors' views, thus creating communities of political homogeneity. Should district lines by drawn in a way that ignores incumbents' residences or the partisanship of the voters?

- *Campaign finance revisited.* Certainly campaign finances play a role. Most challengers are underfunded. Interest groups tend to support incumbents of both parties, because they know incumbents are likely to win. Their contributions, rightly or wrongly, are assumed to guarantee access to decision makers. Can a system be devised that assures challengers a fair chance to raise enough money to compete?

- *Quality of candidates.* The disparity in campaign resources might in fact be a function of the poor quality of those seeking to oppose incumbents. If better candidates were to seek office, they would be able to raise more money and run more competitive races. How one defines "better" candidates is subjective, but by any definition the vast majority of those who do seek to run fall short. Parties spend a good deal of time recruiting candidates who they feel can run competitive races, often only to be turned down. Can means be devised to encourage more qualified candidates to seek office? What incentives would lead those who currently decided not to run to make the opposite decision?

Campaign discourse

We turn finally to the quality of what is said in a campaign. For campaigns to approach the democratic ideal, candidates must voice positions on the most salient issues of the day. The voters must hear these positions and decide among them.

Scholars differ as to how precise the discussion of issues must be. Some claim that candidates must be explicit about their views and that voters must understand these differences, have a preference, and vote on that preference in order for democratic tenets to be met. Others feel that less is needed, that citizens need only have a general impression of whether they feel the country is moving in the right direction and a sense of whom they credit or blame for the direction the country is heading. In either case, voters must get enough information about an incumbent's record and the challenger as an alternative so that they can have an impression and vote on that impression.

- *Negative campaigning.* Too often these differences are expressed through campaigning perceived by voters to be negative. How one defines the term is critical. If one criticizes a series of votes that a legislator has cast on social welfare spending, is that negative? Or is it appropriate criticism? If one criticizes an incumbent for failing

to attend committee sessions, implying that he or she is not doing the job effectively, is that negative or merely relevant criticism? What if one voices this criticism in a belittling manner, pretending to send a search party to look for the absent legislator? Is that too negative or merely using humor to make a point? What if the legislator missed one committee meeting because he or she was in fact attending another, scheduled at the same time? Is it necessary for the critic to point this out, or is it the duty of the person whose attendance has been questioned to correct the record? Is it legitimate to raise a five-year-old DUI conviction during a campaign, if the drunk driving occurred before the candidate was a public servant? What if it was while he or she was in office? What if it was thirty years ago? Are these matters merely personal, or do they reflect on the kind of person we want representing us in office? If potential candidates and citizens are deterred from participating in the process because of negative campaigning, can effective limits be devised without abridging legitimate free political speech?

- *Media coverage of campaigns.* Citizens receive information about political campaigns from two sources, paid media from the candidates and their surrogates, a source directly related to the financial resources of a campaign, and free, supposedly unbiased media, from mass communication outlets. Critics claim that the mass-media campaign coverage fails to provide citizens with adequate information for two reasons—it does not cover campaigns extensively nor does it cover substantive issues in sufficient depth.

Citizens who are determined to know the details of a candidate's record and platform can find that information. However, it requires significant effort, going to a website and searching for the information, steps not likely to be taken by the average voter. The mass media provide very little of this information because they have neither the resources nor the financial incentives to do so.

Even if they did, the networks, the local stations, and local newspapers cannot cover all of the campaigns. The networks give

a great deal of attention to presidential campaigns and spotlight key senatorial, gubernatorial, and congressional races. Local stations and newspapers face an even more difficult problem. They are understaffed and faced with more races to cover. Do they focus on national or statewide races, on local congressional races that might or might not be competitive, on races for state legislature, or on local races? Frequently they are all happening at the same time. If they cover them all, none will get much coverage. Are there innovative ways in which the mass media can be used to better inform the citizenry? Is it the obligation of the media or of the polity to find and to finance such innovations?

Conclusions

The goal of this chapter has not been to depress or infuriate the reader who believes passionately in American democracy. Rather it is to assure that the many virtues of American democracy are not seen without due attention to its flaws.

The United States receives perfect scores on Freedom House's indicators of political rights. Freedom House is an independent NGO that supports democracy and freedom through the world. Americans take pride in a system that encourages political competition, equal participation by all citizens, and citizen control over the government. Opponents can and do openly criticize those in power. When incumbents lose, they leave office and peacefully turn over power to those who have beaten them. And this representative process has flourished for more than two centuries, a period of citizen rule unequaled in human history.

However, although citizens have the right—and some would say the obligation—to participate, many do not. And even though the political process is open for any eligible citizen to run, few in fact have the opportunity to do so. The nominating process is often difficult to understand and results in less than ideal candidates. Although parties have the right to contest for all offices, often they do

not, or they run shadow campaigns with no real opportunity to win. Although citizens are equal in their access to government, money is a huge factor in determining who will be in government and who will have influence on those elected. Although we claim to favor majority rule, our system rarely produces majority winners—and we know little about the second choices of those who support losers. And finally, even though we have free and unfettered political speech, citizens rarely hear candidates discuss the issues of the day in sufficient enough detail to allow for truly informed judgment.

All of these flaws with the system have been noted and addressed by reformers. But solutions are not easy to come by, even if one has the will to do so. It is much easier to point to flaws in a system than to propose solutions that will address those flaws without creating new ones. And in this system, changing the rules of the game requires the consent of those who have attained office under the rules currently in place. In a sense, the foxes are guarding the chicken coop. When citizen dissatisfaction with the system reaches a sufficient level, change occurs. And these changes lead to another cycle of assessment, adjustment, and perhaps further change.

The American electoral process—a two-party system, with separation of powers in a federal system of government—is not a system for all nations. One cannot export culture and traditions. One should not claim perfection for a system that even in the present context has apparent flaws. In extolling the virtues of the electoral system in the United States, one should be as cognizant of its shortcomings as Winston Churchill was of those of British democracy, "It has been said that democracy is the worst form of government except all the others that have been tried." And those who are the strongest advocates for American democracy should be at the forefront of efforts to improve it. In effort after effort to move American democracy toward the ideal, however, few political leaders have put aside their own political interests and focused on the process that would serve the nation best. In fact, that is the test of true leadership.

References

Chapter 2: A brief history of American political parties

The first American political parties: The parties or factions that were feared were the divisions condemned by eighteenth-century British theorists like Lord Bolingbroke ("Governing by party...must always end in government by faction") or David Hume ("Factions subvert government...and beget the fiercest animosities among men of the same nation").

Party system: A party system is the name given to an ongoing electoral situation in which two or more parties compete for power against each other and take each other into account as they govern and set electoral strategies.

Legitimacy of the electoral process: Because of the crisis brought on by the election of 1800, the Constitution was amended to have presidential and vice presidential candidates run as a ticket. It should be noted that the Federalists were well enough organized in 1800 that one of their electors did not vote for Adams's designated running mate, Charles C. Pinckney, but rather for John Jay, precisely to avoid the possibility of a tie vote should Adams have prevailed.

Democratic-Republicans in 1820: Such was the dominance of the Democratic-Republicans that one of their electors voted against James Monroe for reelection as president in 1820, because he wanted Washington to remain the only president to have been chosen unanimously.

The 1824 election: States retained the right to determine how electors were chosen. More and more states were moving away from a

choice by state legislators to popular vote. The election of 1824 is the first for which popular vote totals are available, with approximately 350,000 white males voting.

The 1896 election: Political scientists, following V. O. Key, look at particular elections as critical elections, because the electorate is energized and concerned about its results. Some elections have been labeled as realigning elections, because the ways in which the party coalitions are aligned change significantly. The elections of 1828 (with the emergence of the popular Jackson Democrats and the Whigs as the main rivals), 1860 (with the Republicans and Democrats clashing over the issue of slavery), 1896 (with the parties staying the same but the key issue becoming an economic issue that led to a change in electoral coalitions), and 1932 (with the parties' responses to the Great Depression causing another electoral coalition shift, while the two parties remained the same) are normally listed as the important realigning elections in American history. Others claim that this history is better understood as realigning eras, with these elections merely as convenient points to view ways in which the electorate is shifting.

The Washington precedent: The "Washington precedent" was formalized in the Twenty-second Amendment to the Constitution, ratified in 1951. A reaction to Roosevelt's four terms, the amendment limited future presidents to two full terms.

Parties as a means to organize the government: V. O. Key also is credited with drawing attention to the tripartite nature of party—as organization, in government, and in the electorate. The connections among the three aspects of party were strongest in the gilded age, but they remain important to analyze even today.

Party organizations remained in existence, but their power was gone: In fact, in 1964, Neil Cotter and Bernard Hennessy wrote a book about the two national party committees titled *Politics Without Power*, and in 1971 David Broder, Pulitzer Prize–winning reporter and columnist for the *Washington Post*, published a widely acclaimed analysis of party politics titled *The Party's Over*.

Bible study: And, of course, the irony of Thurmond's life was complete, when it was revealed that he had an illegitimate daughter by an African American woman, a daughter he had been supporting while touting racist views in public life.

Chapter 3: Party organizations: What do they look like? What do they do?

Incumbents run without any major party opposition: In 2002, eighty incumbents won reelection to the U.S. House of Representatives without opposition; in 2004, sixty-five. The recent high was in 1996, when ninety-four incumbents were unopposed.

$5,000 for House candidates and $35,000 for Senate candidates: State parties can also give up to $5,000 to each candidate for federal office, in effect raising the contribution limit from national parties that simply transfer the money to the states.

Leaders of the Hill committees: This section has concentrated on House races rather than Senate races. Much the same process goes on in Senate races. However, because all 435 seats in the House of Representatives are up for election every two years, but only one-third of the Senate seats are being contested, the resource allocation problem is more acute and more significant for the House Hill committees.

Formal structure of party organizations: It should come as no surprise that there is considerable variation from state to state in terms of formal structure.

The conventions of the two national parties set the rules: The two major parties differ somewhat on this point. For the Republicans, rules set at one quadrennial convention remain in effect and cannot be altered until the next convention. For the Democrats, since 1970, party commissions and at times the national committee have been able to modify the rules between conventions. Republican party rules tend to leave more leeway for states to differ in their procedures than do the Democrats' rules, which often restrain state autonomy. These differences reflect philosophical differences between the parties regarding the primacy of state or national governance.

Kickoff to the fall campaign: One variant on this theme deals with those states in which delegates to the national convention are chosen by state conventions, even though no statewide nominations are determined. In these cases, the extent of party unity will vary according to the acrimony among the presidential contenders—and that will often be a function of the timing of the convention within the presidential nominating calendar.

Chapter 4: Who are Republicans? Who are Democrats? Who are the "others"?

Party identification: Scholars now agree that party identification is not totally independent of short-term events of the day, for example, popular candidates or political scandals. However, party ID is generally conceived to be a long-term predilection toward one party or the other that persists despite election specific events. In other words, self-reported partisan attachment is a more accurate measure than voting behavior at any one point in time.

Commercial pollsters: For purposes of predicting who will win an election, pollsters must distinguish between those respondents likely to vote and those less likely to do so. To understand the partisan leanings of the electorate, however, such a distinction is not necessary. In fact, one important research question that focuses on the quality of representation in the United States deals with whether more Republican or Democratic partisans in the total electorate actually turn out to vote.

Party affiliation: The NES question goes on to ask respondents who reply that they consider themselves in one party or the other if they are a strong or a weak supporter of that party, and to ask those who say they consider themselves independent if they lean one way or the other. This analysis, following that of Harold Stanley and Richard Niemi, "Partisanship, Party Coalitions, and Group Support," relies on only the first question.

Party identification of particular groups in society: Analyzing the party identification of members of particular demographic or socioeconomic groups is complex. Most of us are "members" of more than one group. One might be a white southerner, a Catholic, and a union member. These group affiliations pull in different directions. In this analysis, group membership refers to the mean probability that some in a particular group will identify with a political party. Through multiple regression techniques, it is also possible to state how much more likely an individual is to identify with a party because of some particular trait than the same individual would be with all of his or her relevant characteristics *except* that trait. Where appropriate, we will mention Stanley and Niemi's analysis of these contributions as well.

Competing group allegiance: Hispanics in the United States come from a number of different backgrounds—Puerto Rico, Mexico, Cuba, and other countries in Latin America. Cuban Americans, heavily

concentrated in Florida, have had a historical allegiance to the Republican Party, based on the party's policy stands toward Castro.

Black contribution to party coalitions: Of course, black Catholics would count in each of these percentages; the categories are not mutually exclusive.

It is possible to view public opinion on political issues along a spectrum from conservative on the right to liberal on the left: This assumption is certainly an oversimplification of the actual spectrum of public opinion at a time when many complex issues are on the political agenda, and when a conservative stance on one does not necessarily imply a conservative stance on another. With this caveat, the assumption is still useful in understanding how political activists can be distinguished from rank-and-file party identifiers.

Party Unity Score: Party Unity Scores are the percentage of time that a representative votes with his or her party on those votes on which a majority of one party votes together against a majority of the other party.

Republicans opposing a large portion of his initiatives: CQ also computes a Presidential Support and a Presidential Opposition Score. As one would imagine, Democrats in both houses of Congress tend to support President Obama overwhelmingly and oppose him rarely; for Republicans, one sees the opposite pattern.

Chapter 5: Presidential elections: Nominating campaigns and general elections

Typology of competition for presidential nominations: The nominating rules changed significantly after the 1968 presidential election. The thrust of the reforms was to make the process more democratic and less in control of party leaders. This analysis examines only the postreform era.

"Out" party nomination: Throughout this section I discuss only major party nominations. Third or minor party candidacies are at times important in American presidential elections and will be discussed below. Internal politics within the non-major parties, however, will not be discussed, as they are often sui generis, without lessons that can carry to the future.

Presumptive nominee: The definitions of "presumptive nominee" and "serious contenders" in table 5.1 are clearly subjective. "Presumptive nominees" were distinguished from mere front-runners if the media

analysis generally concluded that the nomination was assumed for that candidate...unless someone else could upend him. "Serious contenders" was defined broadly as well-known party leaders or officeholders who received votes in some primary contests. Those who entered primaries but did not fare well are included, but those who were often mentioned or even declared but never entered a primary are not.

The delegates routinely vote for the candidate for vice president suggested to them by the presidential candidate: The most recent exception to that rule was in 1956 when Democratic nominee Adlai Stevenson allowed the convention to choose his running mate. Other nominee choices have been challenged on the floor, but none of their nominations has ever been in serious doubt.

Democratic National Conventions are generally larger than Republican National Conventions: Rules for selection of delegates to the national conventions can be found on the parties' websites, www. democrats.org for the Democrats and www.rnc.org for the Republicans.

Guidelines on state leaders: Philosophical differences among the parties are seen in the party rules. The Republicans believe more in states' rights and give near total discretion to their state units. The Democrats believe more in central control. In addition, as noted in chapter 3, the Republicans believe that the convention is the only sovereign body for the party, thus the only party empowered to impose rules on the party. The Democrats cede some of that power to party commissions and/or to the national committee.

Percentage of votes received in the primary: The Democrats have a minimal percentage or threshold that a candidate must receive in order to win any delegates; that number has varied over the years and is currently set at 15 percent. Front-runners want a higher threshold, and upstart candidates want a lower threshold in order to win some delegates even while trailing badly in the voting.

Proportional representation: To confuse the matter further, in some states the rules for primaries are set in state law; in other states they are left for the parties to determine themselves. Thus, in Michigan in 2004, for example, the Democrats used one system and the Republicans another.

Unified party: A third variation among primary systems deals with who selects the actual delegates to the convention and with the extent to which these delegates remain pledged to the primary winner. Generally the presidential candidate either selects the candidates

for delegate who will run on his or her slate, or the presidential candidate names the actual delegates after the votes have been cast and the number of delegates to be selected has been determined. Delegates from most states are pledged to the candidate for whom they have been chosen for one or two ballots at the convention or until that candidate is no longer running. That last provision is particularly important in the preconvention stage of the nominating process, as delegates pledged to a candidate who drops out (because of lack of overall support) become free agents, ripe for the plucking by the remaining candidates. How delegates for candidates who have dropped out would vote at a convention that went more than one ballot is an unanswered question over which political scientists and political journalists swoon.

The rest were chosen in caucuses: In the Democratic party, some of the delegates, the so-called superdelegates, are chosen because of formal positions they hold and are selected by their peers, for example, members of Congress.

The supporters of either party: In an effort to alleviate this concern, at least partially, the Democrats have changed their rules for the 2008 nomination to allow a limited number of caucus states, with populations more representative of the nation and of the party, to move up their delegate selection dates.

Clinton's initial monetary advantage: Candidates must reach a threshold of donations received, in relatively small individual contributions from a significant of individuals spread throughout a number of states, in order to qualify for matching funds. Once the level has been achieved, the government matches contributions of under $250. If a candidate accepts public money, however, he or she must agree to restrictions on how much money will be spent in campaigning both in individual states and overall.

2000 nomination of George W. Bush: The one early exception was former Texas governor and secretary of the treasury, John Connally, who thought that he could not win the Republican nomination in 1980 unless he significantly outspent his rivals. He raised over $12 million, largely from his Texas oil friends, but still fared extremely poorly, eventually winning only one delegate to the convention. In 1996 millionaire publisher Malcolm "Steve" Forbes also funded his own campaign, making what was seen as a quixotic candidacy more realistic; that experience alerted campaign operatives to a possibility that was exploited in 2000 by George W. Bush.

Hanging chad: Immediately after the election, the United States Congress and many state legislatures began to look at the ballot and the physical means through which Americans vote. While these changes are important, they are largely technical in nature. There is no philosophical argument holding that flawed ballots are good.

No elector may hold any other office of trust under the Constitution: Many do not realize that, even today, electors are actual people who physically go to their state capitols to cast their votes for president.

Cast their votes accordingly: In Maine and Nebraska, state law stipulates that the elector pledged to the popular winner of the vote in each congressional district will win that election and cast one vote for president, and the two electors pledged to the winner of the statewide popular vote win that election and cast the other two votes.

Reconstituted party system: Most Americans are surprised to learn that only five of the last ten presidential elections have resulted in the winning candidates receiving a majority of the votes cast, though all except for George W. Bush in 2000 won a plurality. Even with minor party candidates playing a relatively lesser role in American elections, they have denied a presidential candidate a majority by splintering the vote far more often than not.

One group of reformers, spearheaded by FairVote, a project of the Center for Voting and Democracy, calls for instant runoff voting, a system through which voters rank candidates and their votes are automatically cast for their highest remaining candidate if their first choice is not among the top two finishers. Such a system, which has been adopted in some communities, would solve the runoff problem, but, while this reform idea is gaining adherents, it is far from widely accepted.

Reaching a decisive result in a relatively short time: The election of 2000 and the election of 1876, which also had to be resolved many weeks after the votes were counted, are the two principal exceptions.

Campaign visits: The notable exceptions were California and New York, where candidates often stopped for fund-raising events.

Chapter 6: Subnational nominations and elections

The party selects its nominee: Minor parties, which often have few enrolled members, are given the option of choosing nominees by party caucuses or conventions in most states. In addition, in a few states, the major parties nominate by caucus or convention for at least some offices, though there is often a provision for challenging the nominee chosen in a party meeting through a primary election. Connecticut is an example of a state with such a system.

Voting in primary elections: One often sees reference to the "independent party." Independents are called that because they are independent of party affiliation. Some candidates have formed an "independent party" to capture those dissatisfied with the major parties, but normally the term refers to those who are not enrolled in any political party.

Democrats for the Democratic nomination: Exceptions do exist to this rule. In New York State, for example, state law permits a political party's relevant committee to permit someone registered in another party to seek the first party's nomination. This strategy is often used by minor parties that seek commitments from candidates on specific issues in exchange for their nomination or under threat of withholding that nomination. Often Republicans run not only on their party's line but also as Conservatives or as candidates of the Right-to-Life Party. Democrats seek the Working Families party nod. The candidate's vote in the elections in New York is the total number of votes received on all lines on the ballot.

In 2014 thirty-six governorships were on the ballot: Five states—Kentucky, Louisiana, Mississippi, New Jersey, and Virginia—hold their statewide elections in odd-numbered years; thus the elections correspond with neither presidential nor off-year congressional elections. Two states—New Hampshire and Vermont—elect governors to two-year terms; the other states' governors serve four-year terms.

Term limits: Thirty-six states limit their governors' tenure in office, all to two terms except for Virginia, in which the limit is one term. Some states allow governors to serve again after having left office for at least one term.

Chapter 7: Far from the perfect democracy

Democracies sorted by turnout: Data were collected by the International Institute for Democracy and Electoral Assistance and ranks countries that have had two or more elections since 1945 according to the average turnout (based on voting age population) of all elections. The United States places 114th out of 140 democracies; for the complete data set go to www.idea.int/vt/survey/voter_turnout_pop2-2.cfm.

Registration laws: Various reform efforts have sought to address the problem of low voter turnout in the United States. The most successful of those efforts has been the Voting Rights Act of 1965, most recently renewed for another twenty-five years, which imposed federal standards on states and regions within states that had been shown to discriminate on the basis of race. Ample evidence points to the success of this legislation in raising registration, voting, and office-holding among African Americans. In 1993, after an extended debate, the Congress passed and President Clinton signed the Motor Voter Bill, an act to ease voter registration. While the process has been eased, the result has not been the dramatic increases in registration and voting that were anticipated.

Voting is mandatory: These countries range from Australia, with very strict enforcement, to Bolivia and the Netherlands, with virtually no enforcement. However, those countries in which voting is compulsory by statute, regardless of the sanctions or enforcement mechanisms, vote in higher percentages than do those without such a requirement.

Person-to-person politics: The Democratic party has attempted to reform the process frequently, most recently in 2006, when Nevada was permitted to hold its caucuses between the date of the Iowa caucus and the New Hampshire primary, and South Carolina was allowed to move its primary date to one week after New Hampshire's. That change was a compromise that satisfied no one and was not viewed as addressing the fundamental process.

Front-loading of the process: To be fair, there is little agreement about how it should be changed. If one party's nominee is known in advance, as when a sitting president seeks reelection, the other party benefits if its candidate can secure the nomination early as well. Then the out-party candidate can concentrate on the general

election campaign, rather than defending itself against charges from people within his or her own party.

Electoral College system: In addition to moving to direct election of the president, others have suggested allocating electoral votes proportionately or by districts, as is done in Maine and Nebraska. In 2006 reformers, led by the Center for Voting and Democracy and former third-party presidential candidate John Anderson, proposed changing the system without a constitutional amendment. Their proposal called for states to enter into a compact so that all of the signatory states would agree to cast their electoral votes for the winner of the national vote; the compact would go into effect once enough states had agreed to the compact so that they controlled a majority of the Electoral College. This reform was taken seriously enough that it was endorsed by the *New York Times*, in a lead editorial on March 14, 2006. That the proposal was seriously put forth and that an institution as serious as the *New York Times* would endorse it are clear signs of systemic problems. A fundamental aspect of the constitutional process for selecting the president should not be altered by a means that is, by design, going around the Constitution. On what basis does a constitutional democracy flourish if finding a loophole is considered the legitimate means to effect fundamental change? At the same time, however, that serious people are frustrated enough to consider such an effort signifies that the system itself is in need of reform. And the politicians in charge are not likely to take a reform effort seriously unless the people force them to do so.

$100,000,000 per candidate: Enough early readers of this book have asked whether an extra zero was added to that number in error that I feel compelled to repeat here—$100,000,000.

Free expression of political beliefs: A closely related question is whether such regulation is possible. In 2006, as the House of Representatives debated an effort to plug the loophole through which 527 groups entered the process, Rep. Mike Pence (R-IN) compared the effort to the "whack-a-mole" carnival game, in which a new mole appears every time the player knocks one down.

Freedom through the world: Freedom House's definition of democratic and free governments and ratings of various governments can be found at www.freedomhouse.org.

Further reading

Chapter 1: The context of American elections and political parties

Bibby, John F., and L. Sandy Maisel. *Two Parties or More? The American Party System*. 2nd ed. Boulder, CO: Westview Press, 2002.

Black, Earl, and Merle Black. *The Rise of Southern Republicans*. Cambridge, MA: Harvard University Press, 2004.

Hacker, Andrew. *Congressional Redistricting: The Issue of Equal Representation*. Washington, DC: Brookings Institution, 1964.

Maisel, L. Sandy, and Mark D. Brewer. *Parties and Elections in America: The Electoral Process*, 6th ed. Lanham, MD: Rowman & Littlefield, 2012.

Wolfinger, Raymond E., and Steven J. Rosenstone. *Who Votes?* New Haven: Yale, CT: 1980.

Chapter 2: A brief history of American political parties

Aldrich, John H. *Why Parties? A Second Look*. Chicago: University of Chicago Press, 2011.

Chambers, William Nesbit, and Walter Dean Burnham, eds. *The American Party Systems: Stages of Political Development*. New York: Oxford University Press, 1975.

Gienapp, William E. *The Origins of the Republican Party, 1852–1856*. New York: Oxford University Press, 1987.

Hofstadter, Richard. *The Age of Reform: From Bryan to F.D.R.* New York: Knopf, 1955.

Key, V. O., Jr. *Politics, Parties, and Pressure Groups*, 5th ed. New York: Crowell, 1964.

Sartori, Giovanni. *Parties and Party Systems: A Framework for Analysis*. New York: Cambridge University Press, 1976.

Silbey, Joel H. *The American Political Nation, 1838–1893*. Stanford, CA: Stanford University Press, 1991.

Sundquist, James. *Dynamics of the Party System: Alignment and Realignment of Political Parties in the United States*. Washington, DC: Brookings Institution, 1983.

Young, James S. *The Washington Community, 1800–1828*. New York: Harcourt, Brace & World, 1966.

Chapter 3: Party organizations: What do they look like? What do they do?

Appleton, Andrew M., and Daniel S. Ward. *State Party Profiles: A Fifty-State Guide to Development, Organization, and Resources*. Washington, DC: Congressional Quarterly, 1997.

Cotter, Cornelius P., et al. *Party Organization in American Politics*. Westport, CT: Praeger, 1984.

Mayhew, David R. *Placing Parties in American Politics: Organization, Electoral Settings, and Government Activity in the Twentieth Century*. Princeton, NJ: Princeton University Press, 1986.

Reichley, James. *The Life of the Parties: A History of American Political Parties*. Lanham, MD: Rowman & Littlefield, 2000.

Riordan, William L. *Plunkitt of Tammany Hall: A Series of Very Plain Talks on Very Practical Politics*. Edited by Terrence J. McDonald. New York: Bedford/St. Martin's, 1993.

Chapter 4: Who are Republicans? Who are Democrats? Who are the "others"?

Campbell, Angus, Philip E. Converse, Warren E. Miller, and Donald A. Stokes. *The American Voter*. New York: Wiley, 1960.

Key, V. O., Jr. *Politics, Parties, and Pressure Groups*, 5th ed. New York: Crowell, 1964.

Miller, Warren E., and J. Merrill Shanks., *The New American Voter*. Cambridge, MA: Harvard University Press, 1996.

American Political Parties and Elections

Rapoport, Ronald B., and Walter J. Stone. *Three's a Crowd: The Dynamic of Third Parties, Ross Perot, and Republican Resurgence*. Ann Arbor: University of Michigan Press, 2005.

Stanley, Harold W., and Richard G. Niemi. "Partisanship, Party Coalitions, and Group Support, 1952–2004." *Presidential Studies Quarterly* 36, no. 2 (June 2006), 172–88.

Chapter 5: Presidential elections: Nominating campaigns and general elections

Cook, Rhodes. *The Presidential Nominating Process*. Lanham, MD: Rowman & Littlefield, 2004.

Mayer, William G., ed. *The Making of the Presidential Candidates*. Lanham, MD: Rowman & Littlefield, 2008.

Polsby, Nelson W., Aaron Wildavsky, Steven E. Schier, and David A. Hopkins. *Presidential Elections: Strategies and Structures of American Politics*, 13th ed. Lanham, MD: Rowman & Littlefield, 2011.

Wayne, Stephen. *The Road to the White House, 2016: The Politics of Presidential Elections*. Boston: Cengage Learning, 2016.

Chapter 6: Subnational nominations and elections

Adkins, Randall E., and David A. Dulio, eds. *Cases in Congressional Elections: Riding the Wave*. New York: Routledge, 2012.

Herrnson, Paul S. *Congressional Elections: Campaigning at Home and in Washington*, 6th ed. Washington, DC: Congressional Quarterly Press, 2012.

Jacobson, Gary C. *The Politics of Congressional Elections*, 8th ed. New York: Pearson, 2013.

Magleby, David. *Financing the 2012 Election*. Washington, DC: Brookings Institution, 2014.

Chapter 7: Far from the perfect democracy

Fiorina, Morris. *Culture War? The Myth of a Polarized America*, 3rd ed. New York: Longman, 2010.

Maisel, L. Sandy, Darrell M. West, and Brett Clifton. *Evaluating Campaign Quality: Can the Electoral Process Be Improved?* New York: Cambridge University Press, 2007.

Wattenberg, Martin. *Is Voting for Young People?*, 3rd ed. New York: Longman, 2010.

Index

S

VERY SHORT INTRODUCTIONS are for anyone wanting a stimulating and accessible way into a new subject. They are written by experts, and have been translated into more than 40 different languages.

The series began in 1995, and now covers a wide variety of topics in every discipline. The VSI library now contains more than 450 volumes—a Very Short Introduction to everything from Indian philosophy to psychology and American history and relativity—and continues to grow in every subject area.

Very Short Introductions available now:

American Political Parties and Elections:
A Very Short Introduction